American Bible Society

The Gospel According to St. Mark in English and Cantonese

American Bible Society

The Gospel According to St. Mark in English and Cantonese

ISBN/EAN: 9783337280321

Printed in Europe, USA, Canada, Australia, Japan

Cover: Foto ©Lupo / pixelio.de

More available books at **www.hansebooks.com**

馬可福音

中西字

THE GOSPEL ACCORDING TO

ST. MARK

IN

ENGLISH AND CANTONESE.

PUBLISHED BY THE

AMERICAN BIBLE SOCIETY.

SHANGHAI:
AMERICAN PRESBYTERIAN MISSION PRESS.
1899.

書音福傳可馬
THE GOSPEL ACCORDING TO MARK.

CHAPTER 1.

THE beginning of the gospel of Jesus Christ, the Son of God;

2 As it is written in the prophets, Behold, I send my messenger before thy face, which shall prepare thy way before thee.

3 The voice of one crying in the wilderness, Prepare ye the way of the Lord, make his paths straight.

4 John did baptize in the wilderness, and preach the baptism of repentance for the remission of sins.

5 And there went out unto him all the land of Judea, and they of Jerusalem, and were all baptized of him in the river of Jordan, confessing their sins.

6 And John was clothed with camel's hair, and with a girdle of a skin about his loins; and he did eat locusts and wild honey;

7 And preached, saying, There cometh one mightier than I after me, the latchet of whose shoes I am not worthy to stoop down and unloose.

8 I indeed have baptized you with water: but he shall baptize you with the Holy Ghost.

第一章

一、神之子耶穌基督福音嘅起首。照先知以賽亞書所載話、我打發我嘅使者在你面前預備你嘅路喺曠野有人聲呼叫話、預備主嘅大路、整直佢嘅小路。約翰喺曠野施洗、宣傳悔改嘅洗禮致罪得赦。通猶大地方、與及耶路撒冷嘅人、都出去佢處、俱認自己罪、喺約但河受約翰施洗。約翰著駱駝毛嘅衫、腰束皮帶、所食嘅係蝗蟲野蜜。佢傳道話有一個後過我嘅嘅、佢能力勝過我、我屈身解佢鞋帶都唔相稱。我用水嚟施洗你哋、但佢將用聖靈施洗你哋嘅。

2   ST. MARK.

9 And it came to pass in those days, that Jesus came from Nazareth of Galilee, and was baptized of John in Jordan.

10 And straightway coming up out of the water, he saw the heavens opened, and the Spirit like a dove descending upon him:

11 And there came a voice from heaven, *saying*, Thou art my beloved Son, in whom I am well pleased.

12 And immediately the Spirit driveth him into the wilderness.

13 And he was there in the wilderness forty days tempted of Satan; and was with the wild beasts; and the angels ministered unto him.

14 Now after that John was put in prison, Jesus came into Galilee, preaching the gospel of the kingdom of God,

15 And saying, The time is fulfilled and the kingdom of God is at hand: repent ye, and believe the gospel.

16 Now as he walked by the sea of Galilee, he saw Simon and Andrew his brother casting a net into the sea: for they were fishers.

17 And Jesus said unto them, Come ye after me, and I will make you to become fishers of men.

馬可第一章

○當時耶穌自加利利嘅拿撒勒嚟、喺約但河、受約翰施洗。喺水番上嚟、佢就見天開、有聖靈好似白鴿降臨佢身上、又自天有聲話、你係我嘅愛子、我所歡喜嘅。○聖靈即時催耶穌去曠野、佢喺曠野四十日、受撒但試惑、共野獸同住、又有天使嚟服事佢。○約翰坐監之後、耶穌嚟到加利利、傳講 神嘅福音嘅話、日期滿咯、 神國近咯、你哋應該悔改信福音。○耶穌行遊加利利海邊、睇見西門、共佢嘅兄弟安得烈、撒網落海、因佢哋係攞魚嘅人。耶穌對佢哋話跟從我、我將令你哋攞人、好似攞魚一樣。

ST. MARK.

18 And straightway they forsook their nets, and followed him.

19 And when he had gone a little further thence, he saw James the *son* of Zebedee, and John his brother, who also were in the ship mending their nets.

20 And straightway he called them: and they left their father Zebedee in the ship with the hired servants, and went after him.

21 And they went into Capernaum; and straightway on the sabbath day he entered into the synagogue, and taught.

22 And they were astonished at his doctrine: for he taught them as one that had authority, and not as the scribes.

23 And there was in their synagogue a man with an unclean spirit; and he cried out,

24 Saying, Let *us* alone; what have we to do with thee, thou Jesus of Nazareth? art thou come to destroy us? I know thee who thou art, the Holy One of God.

25 And Jesus rebuked him, saying, Holy thy peace, and come out of him.

26 And when the unclean spirit had torn him, and cried with a loud voice, he came out of him.

佢哋即時丟棄個張網、跟從耶穌。○耶穌喺個處行冇遠、又見西庇太嘅仔雅各、及佢兄弟約翰、喺船上補網、耶穌即時叫佢哋、佢就離別父親西庇太與及工人在船上跟耶穌去。○大衆嚟到迦百農、適值安息日耶穌入會堂教人、衆人驚奇佢嘅教訓、因佢教人好似有權柄嘅噉、唔似個的讀書人。適值會堂有個人被邪鬼迷嘅、大聲呼話、拿撒勒人耶穌、我與你何干呢、你嚟想敗壞我哋咩、我知你係乜誰、乃係　神嘅聖者。耶穌責佢話、咪出聲、離開佢出去㗎、邪鬼就使個人縮攣、大叫一聲、離開佢出去。

ST. MARK.

27 And they were all amazed, insomuch that they questioned among themselves, saying, What thing is this? what new doctrine is this? for with authority commandeth he even the unclean spirits, and they do obey him.

28 And immediately his fame spread abroad throughout all the region round about Galilee.

29 And forthwith, when they were come out of the synagogue, they entered into the house of Simon and Andrew, with James and John.

30 But Simon's wife's mother lay sick of a fever; and anon they tell him of her.

31 And he came and took her by the hand, and lifted her up; and immediately the fever left her, and she ministered unto them.

32 And at even, when the sun did set, they brought unto him all that were diseased, and them that were possessed with devils.

33 And all the city was gathered together at the door.

34 And he healed many that were sick of divers diseases, and cast out many devils; and suffered not the devils to speak, because they knew him.

35 And in the morning, rising up a great while before day, he went out, and departed into a solitary place, and there prayed.

眾人見好出奇大家相問話呢的係也嘢呢、係新教訓咯、佢搣權柄吩咐邪鬼、邪鬼就依從佢咯。嘅就耶穌嘅名聲、即時傳勻加利利嘅四方。○佢哋旣出會堂、耶穌共雅各、約翰、入西門安得烈嘅家、西門嘅外母有發熱病倒床處、就有人話耶穌知。耶穌行前、執住佢手拉起佢、熱卽退、個女人就服事佢哋。到挨晚熱頭落之時、眾人帶住凡有病嘅、被鬼所迷嘅嚟到耶穌處。嘅就通城嘅人聚集門前。耶穌醫好好多病人、係有各樣症嘅、及趕好多鬼、因爲個的鬼識佢、故此耶穌唔俾佢出聲。○到第朝天色尙黑、耶穌早早起身出去曠野地方祈禱。

St. Mark.

36 And Simon and they that were with him followed after him.

37 And when they had found him, they said unto him, All *men* seek for thee.

38 And he said unto them, Let us go into the next towns, that I may preach there also: for therefore came I forth.

39 And he preached in their synagogues throughout all Galilee, and cast out devils.

40 And there came a leper to him, beseeching him, and kneeling down to him, and saying unto him, If thou wilt, thou canst make me clean.

41 And Jesus, moved with compassion, put forth *his* hand, and touched him, and saith unto him, I will; be thou clean.

42 And as soon as he had spoken, immediately the leprosy departed from him, and he was cleansed.

43 And he straitly charged him, and forthwith sent him away;

44 And saith unto him, See thou say nothing to any man: but go thy way, shew thyself to the priest, and offer for thy cleansing those things which Moses commanded, for a testimony unto them

西門共同伴嘅人追尋佢。遇着就對佢話、眾人都揾你呀。耶穌對佢哋話、我哋應該去別處、到附近鄉村、等我喺個處傳道、因我喺係為呢樣事呀。就耶穌喺加利利各處會堂傳道逐鬼。○有個癩瘋嘅人嚟求耶穌跪處對佢話、你若係肯就能潔淨我略。耶穌憐憫佢、就伸手摩吓佢、又話我肯你得潔淨路。個人嘅癩瘋卽時用曉全身潔淨。耶穌嚴禁佢、卽時使佢去、又對佢話你至緊唔好講過人知但去俾過祭司睇、因為你得潔淨、要依摩西嘅吩附、獻禮物、俾過眾人做見證。

45 But he went out, and began to publish *it* much, and to blaze abroad the matter, insomuch that Jesus could no more openly enter into the city, but was without in desert places: and they came to him from every quarter.

CHAPTER 2.

AND again he entered into Capernaum after *some* days; and it was noised that he was in the house.

2 And straightway many were gathered together insomuch that there was no room to receive *them*, no, not so much as about the door: and he preached the word unto them.

3 And they come unto him, bringing one sick of the palsy, which was borne of four.

4 And when they could not come nigh unto him for the press, they uncovered the roof where he was: and when they had broken *it* up, they let down the bed wherein the sick of the palsy lay.

5 When Jesus saw their faith, he said unto the sick of the palsy, Son, thy sins be forgiven thee.

6 But there were certain of the scribes sitting there, and reasoning in their hearts,

第二章

一但佢出去就講好多說話傳開呢的事、故此耶穌唔得顯然入城單喺野外居住、四方嘅人喺親就佢。

二過幾日耶穌再入迦百農、人聽見佢喺屋跂就有好多人喺聚集至到門前都冇空地、耶穌就傳道佢哋聽。三有人帶一個瘋癱嘅喺、係四個人擡嘅。四因為人多不能近前、就喺耶穌所在個間屋瓦面拆開一個窿將個瘋癱人、連床弔落去耶穌見佢哋咁信賴佢、就對瘋癱嘅話仔呀、你嘅罪得赦咯。六有幾個讀書人喺處坐、心中議論話、

ST. MARK.

7 Why doth this *man* thus speak blasphemies? who can forgive sins but God only?

8 And immediately, when Jesus perceived in his spirit that they so reasoned within themselves, he said unto them, Why reason ye these things in your hearts?

9 Whether is it easier to say to the sick of the palsy, *Thy* sins be forgiven thee; or to say, Arise, and take up thy bed, and walk?

10 But that ye may know that the Son of man hath power on earth to forgive sins, (he saith to the sick of the palsy,)

11 I say unto thee, Arise, and take up thy bed, and go thy way into thine house.

12 And immediately he arose, took up the bed, and went forth before them all; insomuch that they were all amazed, and glorified God, saying, We never saw it on this fashion.

13 And he went forth again by the sea side; and all the multitude resorted unto him, and he taught them.

14 And as he passed by, he saw Levi the *son* of Alpheus sitting at the receipt of custom, and said unto him, Follow me. And he arose and followed him.

馬可第二章

七呢個人、做乜嘢講呢、佢褻瀆咯、除曉神之外、邊個能赦罪呢、耶穌心中知到佢哋私自議論就對佢哋話你哋心內做乜議論呢、對瘋癱人話你罪得赦抑或話起身摔你張床行去邊樣易呢。但令你哋知到人子喺地上有赦罪嘅權柄。就對個瘋癱人話我叫你起身拈你床去歸、個人在眾人面前起身卽時摔床出去眾人就驚奇歸榮神話我哋總唔曾見過咯嘅事。○耶穌再出去到海邊有羣眾親就佢、耶穌就教訓佢哋又喺呢處行去、睇見亞勒腓子利未坐在稅關、就對佢話跟從我喇佢就起身跟從耶穌。

15 And it came to pass, that, as Jesus sat at meat in his house, many publicans and sinners sat also together with Jesus and his disciples; for there were many, and they followed him.

16 And when the scribes and Pharisees saw him eat with publicans and sinners, they said unto his disciples, How is it that he eateth and drinketh with publicans and sinners?

17 When Jesus heard it, he saith unto them, They that are whole have no need of the physician, but they that are sick: I came not to call the righteous, but sinners to repentance.

18 And the disciples of John and of the Pharisees used to fast: and they come and say unto him, Why do the disciples of John and of the Pharisees fast, but thy disciples fast not?

19 And Jesus said unto them, Can the children of the bridechamber fast, while the bridegroom is with them? as long as they have the bridegroom with them, they cannot fast.

20 But the days will come, when the bridegroom shall be taken away from them, and then shall they fast in those days

耶穌喺利未屋踎坐席、有好多收稅嘅、及有罪嘅人、共耶穌及佢門生同席為個的人多、而且跟從耶穌呀。啦唎嚹中嘅讀書人、見耶穌同收稅嘅、及罪人共食、就對佢門生話佢共收稅嘅及罪人飲食呀。耶穌聽聞對佢哋話壯健嘅人、唔使要醫生、但係有病嘅致要呪、我嚟唔係叫義人悔改、係叫罪人悔改咩。○約翰嘅門生、共唎嚹人、禁食個時、有人嚟對耶穌話、約翰嘅門生、及啦唎嚹人嘅門生都禁食、你門生做乜唔禁食嘅呢。耶穌對佢哋話、新郎喺處之時、賀新郎嘅人、點能禁食呢、重有新郎同埋喺處、個時不能禁食、惟係將來新郎離別佢哋去曉、個陣時就必禁食畧。

21 No man also seweth a piece of new cloth on an old garment; else the new piece that filled it up taketh away from the old, and the rent is made worse.

22 And no man putteth new wine into old bottles; else the new wine doth burst the bottles, and the wine is spilled, and the bottles will be marred: but new wine must be put into new bottles.

23 And it came to pass, that he went through the corn fields on the sabbath day; and his disciples began, as they went, to pluck the ears of corn.

24 And the Pharisees said unto him, Behold, why do they on the sabbath day that which is not lawful?

25 And he said unto them, Have ye never read what David did, when he had need, and was a hungered, he, and they that were with him?

26 How he went into the house of God in the days of Abiathar the high priest, and did eat the shewbread, which is not lawful to eat but for the priests, and gave also to them which were with him?

27 And he said unto them, The sabbath was made for man, and not man for the sabbath:

28 Therefore the Son of man is Lord also of the sabbath.

CHAPTER 3.

AND he entered again into the synagogue; and there was a man there which had a withered hand.

2 And they watched him, whether he would heal him on the sabbath day; that they might accuse him.

3 And he saith unto the man which had the withered hand, Stand forth.

4 And he saith unto them, Is it lawful to do good on the sabbath days, or to do evil? to save life, or to kill? But they held their peace.

5 And when he had looked round about on them with anger, being grieved for the hardness of their hearts, he saith unto the man, Stretch forth thine hand. And he stretched it out: and his hand was restored whole as the other.

6 And the Pharisees went forth, and straightway took counsel with the Herodians against him, how they might destroy him.

7 But Jesus withdrew himself with his disciples to the sea: and a great multitude from Galilee followed him, and from Judea,

第三章

一耶穌再入會堂、有個一隻手乾枯嘅人喺處。二衆人睄住耶穌安息日醫佢唔醫、意係想告訟佢耶穌就對枯手嘅人話起身企在中間又在衆人話喺安息日行善事行惡事救生命殺生命邊樣、衆人冇出聲耶穌惱怒周圍望吓、衆人、因閉翳佢哋嘅心咁硬呀、就對個人話伸開你個隻手喇、佢把手一伸、就好番咯喇嘆人出去、卽時共希律黨個人斟酌、點樣嚟殺耶穌。○耶穌同門生退出去海邊有羣衆喺加利利猶大、

St. Mark.

8 And from Jerusalem, and from Idumea, and *from* beyond Jordan; and they about Tyre and Sidon, a great multitude, when they had heard what great things he did, came unto him.

9 And he spake to his disciples, that a small ship should wait on him because of the multitude, lest they should throng him,

10 For he had healed many; insomuch that they pressed upon him for to touch him, as many as had plagues.

11 And unclean spirits, when they saw him, fell down before him, and cried, saying, Thou art the Son of God.

12 And he straitly charged them that they should not make him known.

13 And he goeth up into a mountain, and calleth *unto him* whom he would: and they came unto him.

14 And he ordained twelve, that they should be with him, and that he might send them forth to preach,

15 And to have power to heal sicknesses, and to cast out devils:

16 And Simon he surnamed Peter;

馬可第三章 11

耶路撒冷以土買約但外嘅、嚟跟從佢、又有好多推羅西頓嘅人、聽聞佢所做嘅事、亦嚟親就佢、耶穌吩咐門生、整定隻小船等佢、免致人多逼佢。因為醫好人多故此凡有病嘅、都逼近佢身想摩吓佢個的邪鬼一見就噗倒佢面前、大聲叫話你係神之子呀。耶穌嚴禁佢哋、唔好將佢講過人知。○耶穌上山、隨自己意嚟叫人、個的人就到佢處。耶穌又設立十二個人、想佢哋跟隨佢、而且打發佢哋傳道亦俾佢哋有趕鬼嘅權有個係西門改佢名做彼得。

12 ST. MARK.

17 And James the *son* of Zebedee, and John the brother of James; and he surnamed them Boanerges, which is, The sons of thunder:

18 And Andrew, and Philip, and Bartholomew, and Matthew, and Thomas, and James the *son* of Alpheus, and Thaddeus, and Simon the Canaanite,

19 And Judas Iscariot, which also betrayed him: and they went into a house.

20 And the multitude cometh together again, so that they could not so much as eat bread.

21 And when his friends heard *of it*, they went out to lay hold on him: for they said, He is beside himself.

22 ¶ And the scribes which came down from Jerusalem said, He hath Beelzebub, and by the prince of the devils casteth he out devils.

23 And he called them *unto him*, and said unto them in parables, How can Satan cast out Satan?

24 And if a kingdom be divided against itself, that kingdom cannot stand.

25 And if a house be divided against itself, that house cannot stand.

26 And if Satan rise up against himself, and be divided, he cannot stand, but hath an end.

St. MARK.

27 No man can enter into a strong man's house, and spoil his goods, except he will first bind the strong man; and then he will spoil his house.

28 Verily I say unto you, All sins shall be forgiven unto the sons of men, and blasphemies wherewith soever they shall blaspheme:

29 But he that shall blaspheme against the Holy Ghost hath never forgiveness, but is in danger of eternal damnation.

30 Because they said, He hath an unclean spirit.

31 ¶ There came then his brethren and his mother, and, standing without, sent unto him, calling him.

32 And the multitude sat about him, and they said unto him, Behold, thy mother and thy brethren without seek for thee.

33 And he answered them, saying, Who is my mother, or my brethren?

34 And he looked round about on them which sat about him, and said, Behold my mother and my brethren!

35 For whosoever shall do the will of God, the same is my brother, and my sister, and mother.

冇人能入勇士嘅屋、搶刼佢家財必要先綁起勇士然後致刼得佢屋我實在話你哋知、世人所有罪惡與及褻瀆嘅話都可以赦得惟係褻瀆聖靈嘅總唔赦得必永遠有罪耶穌因人話佢係邪鬼所迷故此講呢的說話。〇個陣耶穌嘅母親與及佢兄弟嚟企在外便使人入去叫佢、衆人圍住耶穌坐處、有人對佢話你母親及兄弟、喺外便搵你。耶穌答佢哋話邊個係我母親我兄弟呢。就周圍望吓同坐嘅人話請睇我嘅母親、我嘅兄弟吖、但凡遵依神旨意嘅、卽係我兄弟、姊妹、及母親咯。

CHAPTER 4.

AND he began again to teach by the sea side: and there was gathered unto him a great multitude, so that he entered into a ship, and sat in the sea; and the whole multitude was by the sea on the land.

2 And he taught them many things by parables, and said unto them in his doctrine,

3 Hearken; Behold, there went out a sower to sow:

4 And it came to pass, as he sowed, some fell by the way side, and the fowls of the air came and devoured it up.

5 And some fell on stony ground, where it had not much earth; and immediately it sprang up, because it had no depth of earth:

6 But when the sun was up, it was scorched; and because it had no root, it withered away.

7 And some fell among thorns, and the thorns grew up, and choked it, and it yielded no fruit.

8 And other fell on good ground, and did yield fruit that sprang up and increased, and brought forth, some thirty, and some sixty, and some a hundred.

第四章

耶穌再喺海邊敎人、有羣衆喺親佢、哦佢就落船坐處浮在海面、衆人喺海邊企在岸上耶穌設譬喻、搣多端敎佢哋、敎訓之時對衆人話你哋聽呀、有一個撒種嘅人、出去撒種撒個時有的跌落路邊雀鳥喺到食噉。有的跌落石地泥薄個處、因爲泥土唔深發芽好快、但係冇根熱頭出嚟哂佢、就枯槁咯有的跌落荆棘裏頭、荆棘發生起嚟、就偪死佢、唔結得實。有的跌落肥地、發生長大起嚟結實有二十倍有六十倍有一百倍。

ST. MARK.

9 And he said unto them, He that hath ears to hear, let him hear.

10 And when he was alone, they that were about him with the twelve asked of him the parable.

11 And he said unto them, Unto you it is given to know the mystery of the kingdom of God: but unto them that are without, all *these* things are done in parables:

12 That seeing they may see, and not perceive; and hearing they may hear, and not understand; lest at any time they should be converted, and *their* sins should be forgiven them.

13 And he said unto them, Know ye not this parable? and how then will ye know all parables?

14 ¶ The sower soweth the word.

15 And these are they by the way side, where the word is sown; but when they have heard, Satan cometh immediately, and taketh away the word that was sown in their hearts.

16 And these are they likewise which are sown on stony ground; who, when they have heard the word, immediately receive it with gladness;

又話、有耳可聽嘅、就要聽罷。○十耶穌靜坐個時、圍住佢嘅人、共十二門生、搣呢的譬喻問佢。十耶穌對佢哋話、神國嘅奧妙、係俾過你哋、若係外人、就要用譬喻敎佢等。十佢哋雖然睇、都唔明白、雖然聽、都唔曉得、免致佢改變而得罪赦。又對佢哋話、呢的譬喻你都唔曉、點曉得各樣譬喻呢。十撒種嘅、卽係傳道理。十撒落路邊嘅、卽係人聽道理、撒但就隊、將撒在佢心嘅道搶曉。撒落石地嘅、卽係人聽道理就歡喜接受、

ST. MARK.

17 And have no root in themselves, and so endure but for a time: afterward, when affliction or persecution ariseth for the word's sake, immediately they are offended.

18 And these are they which are sown among thorns; such as hear the word,

19 And the cares of this world, and the deceitfulness of riches, and the lusts of other things entering in, choke the word, and it becometh unfruitful.

20 And these are they which are sown on good ground; such as hear the word, and receive *it*, and bring forth fruit, some thirtyfold, some sixty, and some a hundred.

21 ¶ And he said unto them, Is a candle brought to be put under a bushel, or under a bed? and not to be set on a candlestick?

22 For there is nothing hid, which shall not be manifested; neither was any thing kept secret, but that it should come abroad.

23 If any man have ears to hear, let him hear.

24 And he said unto them, Take heed what ye hear. With what measure ye mete, it shall be measured to you; and unto you that hear shall more be given.

但係心內冇根蒂、不過暫時咋、及至爲道有艱難陷害佢就卽時厭棄。撒在荊棘裏頭嘅、卽係人聽道理、有今世嘅掛慮共錢財嘅迷惑與及各樣嘅私慾都嚟侵死道理唔結得實。撒落肥地嘅、卽係人聽道理就接納嘵而且結實起嚟、有三十倍嘅、有六十倍嘅、有一百倍嘅。○耶穌又對佢哋話人攞燈嚟、豈係擠落斗下、或床下嘅咩、唔係擠在燈臺上嘅咩。因爲總有隱密嘅事將來唔顯現、藏埋嘅事將來唔露出嚟但凡有耳可聽嘅、就要聽呀。又對佢哋話你哋要謹愼所聽呀、你點樣量度人人亦必啦樣量度你、而且是必加多賜過你。

ST. MARK.

25 For he that hath, to him shall be given; and he that hath not, from him shall be taken even that which he hath.

26 ¶ And he said, So is the kingdom of God, as if a man should cast seed into the ground;

27 And should sleep, and rise night and day, and the seed should spring and grow up, he knoweth not how.

28 For the earth bringeth forth fruit of herself; first the blade, then the ear, after that the full corn in the ear.

29 But when the fruit is brought forth, immediately he putteth in the sickle, because the harvest is come.

30 ¶ And he said, Whereunto shall we liken the kingdom of God? or with what comparison shall we compare it?

31 It is like a grain of mustard seed, which, when it is sown in the earth, is less than all the seeds that be in the earth:

32 But when it is sown, it groweth up, and becometh greater than all herbs, and shooteth out great branches; so that the fowls of the air may lodge under the shadow of it.

33 And with many such parables spake he the word unto them, as they were able to hear it.

因爲有嘅、重要加添過佢、冇嘅、就連佢所有都要奪番。○又話、神嘅國好比人撒種落地、佢日間起、夜間瞓、個的種發芽長大、個人都唔知佢點得嘅樣。地土自然能結實嘅、始初係秧、漸漸成穗、及後穗上結滿穀已經長熟、就用鐮刀、因爲收割嘅時候到咯。○又話、神嘅國好比也嘢呢、我哋設也野譬喻嚟解明佢呢、好似一粒芥菜仁、撒落地個時、係世上百樣仁之中至細嘅、撒落之後就發起嚟、大過各樣嘅菜、而且生出的枝好大至到空中雀鳥可以住在佢陰處耶穌又用好多噉嘅譬喻對衆人傳道、係照依佢哋所能聽嘅。

ST. MARK.　　　　馬可第四章

34 But without a parable spake he not unto them: and when they were alone, he expounded all things to his disciples.

35 And the same day, when the even was come, he saith unto them, Let us pass over unto the other side.

36 And when they had sent away the multitude, they took him even as he was in the ship. And there were also with him other little ships.

37 And there arose a great storm of wind, and the waves beat into the ship, so that it was now full.

38 And he was in the hinder part of the ship, asleep on a pillow: and they awake him, and say unto him, Master, carest thou not that we perish?

39 And he arose, and rebuked the wind, and said unto the sea, Peace, be still. And the wind ceased, and there was a great calm.

40 And he said unto them, Why are ye so fearful? how is it that ye have no faith?

41 And they feared exceedingly, and said one to another, What manner of man is this, that even the wind and the sea obey him?

三十四唔係譬喻就唔對眾人講、到淨係佢哋喺個時、佢解明曬過門生聽。○個日挨晚時耶穌對門生話我哋要過個便岸嘅、就叫門生散曉眾人耶穌仍然喺船上佢哋就共佢過海另外有別隻船同行、即有狂風大起、浪打入船將近滿咯。耶穌喺船尾椓住枕頭瞓瞓門生叫醒佢、就對佢話老師、我哋死咯你都唔顧咩。耶穌起身喝個的風對住海話平靜喇、咪搖動路、個的風就止息海極平靜。耶穌就對門生話、你哋使乜慌呢、未曾有信德咩。佢哋好驚慌、大家相講話呢個係乜嘢人呢、風共海亦順從佢呀。

ST. MARK.　　　　馬可第五章　19

CHAPTER 5.

AND they came over unto the other side of the sea, into the country of the Gadarenes.

2 And when he was come out of the ship, immediately there met him out of the tombs a man with an unclean spirit,

3 Who had *his* dwelling among the tombs; and no man could bind him, no, not with chains:

4 Because that he had been often bound with fetters and chains, and the chains had been plucked asunder by him, and the fetters broken in pieces: neither could any *man* tame him.

5 And always, night and day, he was in the mountains, and in the tombs, crying, and cutting himself with stones.

6 But when he saw Jesus afar off, he ran and worshipped him,

7 And cried with a loud voice, and said, What have I to do with thee, Jesus, *thou* Son of the most high God? I adjure thee by God, that thou torment me not.

8 (For he said unto him, Come out of the man, *thou* unclean spirit.)

第五章

佢哋過海、到個便岸加拉沙嘅地方耶穌離開個隻船、即時有一個被邪鬼迷嘅人、喺墳墓出嚟遇着佢。呢個人喺墳墓裏住、人雖搣鎖鍊都唔鎖得住佢。因爲屢次搣脚鐐鎖鍊鎖佢、佢扭斷鎖鍊、搣爛脚鐐總冇人制服得佢、日夜常在山上墳墓叫喊、又用石嚟傷自己遠遠望見耶穌就走前拜佢。大聲叫話至高神子耶穌、我與你何干呢我托神名懇求你、唔好令我受苦因爲耶穌也曾對佢話邪鬼呀喺個人處出嚟喇。

ST. MARK.

9 And he asked him, What *is* thy name? And he answered, saying, My name *is* Legion: for we are many.

10 And he besought him much that he would not send them away out of the country.

11 Now there was there nigh unto the mountains a great herd of swine feeding.

12 And all the devils besought him, saying, Send us into the swine, that we may enter into them.

13 And forthwith Jesus gave them leave. And the unclean spirits went out, and entered into the swine; and the herd ran violently down a steep place into the sea, (they were about two thousand,) and were choked in the sea.

14 And they that fed the swine fled, and told *it* in the city, and in the country. And they went out to see what it was that was done.

15 And they come to Jesus, and see him that was possessed with the devil, and had the legion, sitting, and clothed, and in his right mind; and they were afraid.

16 And they that saw *it* told them how it befell to him that was possessed with the devil, and *also* concerning the swine.

17 And they began to pray him to depart out of their coasts.

馬可第五章

耶穌就問佢話你叫乜名佢話我名叫軍因為我哋係多呀佢就懇求耶穌唔好趕佢哋離開個處地方㗎個處山邊有一大隊豬食緊嘢衆鬼求佢哋話打發我哋去個隊豬處等我哋入佢嚟頭罷喇耶穌就准佢哋邪鬼出曉入去豬處成隊豬都跑落山坡投入海中咷死其數大約二千隻看豬嘅人走去話過城裏共鄉下嘅人知衆人就求耶穌離開佢嘅境地。

ST. MARK.

18 And when he was come into the ship, he that had been possessed with the devil prayed him that he might be with him.

19 Howbeit Jesus suffered him not, but saith unto him, Go home to thy friends, and tell them how great things the Lord hath done for thee, and hath had compassion on thee.

20 And he departed, and began to publish in Decapolis how great things Jesus had done for him: and all *men* did marvel.

21 And when Jesus was passed over again by ship unto the other side, much people gathered unto him; and he was nigh unto the sea.

22 And, behold, there cometh one of the rulers of the synagogue, Jairus by name; and when he saw him, he fell at his feet,

23 And besought him greatly, saying, My little daughter lieth at the point of death: *I pray thee,* come and lay thy hands on her, that she may be healed; and she shall live.

24 And *Jesus* went with him; and much people followed him, and thronged him.

25 And a certain woman, which had an issue of blood twelve years,

26 And had suffered many things of many physicians, and had spent all that she had, and was nothing bettered, but rather grew worse,

---

馬可第五章

耶穌落船之時、先頭被鬼迷個人、求耶穌准佢同埋去。但耶穌唔准、就對佢話、你去歸、見你家人將主爲你做咁大嘅事、及憐憫你嘅、講過佢哋聽。個人就去曉、在低加波利、傳開耶穌爲佢做咁大嘅事、衆人見出奇。○耶穌坐船再過個便岸有羣衆聚集喺處、佢正在海邊。有一個管理會堂嘅人名叫做睚魯、見耶穌、撲倒佢腳下、懇切求話、我小女將近死、請你嚟、撳手按吓佢、令佢好番、就是必得生略。耶穌就同佢去、好多人跟隨佢、而且擠擁住佢。有個女人血漏十二年、受過好多醫生嘅苦楚、佢嘅家財都唔見好的、而且病症越發重、

ST. MARK.

27 When she had heard of Jesus, came in the press behind, and touched his garment.

28 For she said, If I may touch but his clothes, I shall be whole.

29 And straightway the fountain of her blood was dried up; and she felt in *her* body that she was healed of that plague.

30 And Jesus, immediately knowing in himself that virtue had gone out of him, turned him about in the press, and said, Who touched my clothes?

31 And his disciples said unto him, Thou seest the multitude thronging thee, and sayest thou, Who touched me?

32 And he looked round about to see her that had done this thing.

33 But the woman fearing and trembling, knowing what was done in her, came and fell down before him, and told him all the truth.

34 And he said unto her, Daughter, thy faith hath made thee whole; go in peace, and be whole of thy plague.

35 While he yet spake, there came from the ruler of the synagogue's *house certain* which said, Thy daughter is dead; why troublest thou the Master any further?

36 As soon as Jesus heard the word that was spoken, he saith unto the ruler of the synagogue, Be not afraid, only believe.

聞得耶穌嘅事、就喺佢後便衆人之中、喺摩吓佢衫、因爲佢話、我單係摩吓佢衫、就必定得好嘅、佢嘅血漏立刻止曉、覺得身內嘅病好嘅。耶穌卽時覺得有奇能喺自己處出、就在衆人之中、陟轉身話、也誰摩我件衫呢、門生對佢話、你見衆人擠擁你、重問也誰摩我咩、耶穌周圍望吓、想見做呢件事嘅女人、個女人知到本身得好曉、就好慌也震、噗倒佢面前、照實講嘅過佢知、但耶穌對佢話、女呀、你嘅信德救曉你、可以安樂去歸喇、你嘅病好嘅咯。〇佢講緊個時、有的人喺管理會堂嘅家中嚟、話、你女死曉咯、徒也重勞動老師呢。耶穌一聞佢哋所講、就對管理會堂嘅話、唔使慌、獨係要信咃、

St. Mark.

37 And he suffered no man to follow him, save Peter, and James, and John the brother of James.
38 And he cometh to the house of the ruler of the synagogue, and seeth the tumult, and them that wept and wailed greatly.
39 And when he was come in, he saith unto them, Why make ye this ado, and weep? the damsel is not dead, but sleepeth.
40 And they laughed him to scorn. But when he had put them all out, he taketh the father and the mother of the damsel, and them that were with him, and entereth in where the damsel was lying.
41 And he took the damsel by the hand, and said unto her, Talitha cumi; which is, being interpreted, Damsel, (I say unto thee,) arise.
42 And straightway the damsel arose, and walked; for she was *of the age* of twelve years. And they were astonished with a great astonishment.
43 And he charged them straitly that no man should know it; and commanded that something should be given her to eat.

CHAPTER 6.

AND he went out from thence, and came into his own country; and his disciples follow him.

嘅、就除曉彼得雅各及雅各兄弟約翰之外、唔准別人跟佢、到曉管理會堂嘅屋跡、見好嘈雜、有人啼哭悲哀得好淒涼耶穌已經入去對佢哋話、爲乜咁嘈雜啼哭呢、個女仔唔係死、不過瞓着咗、衆人就笑佢耶穌打發佢哋出去、帶住個女仔嘅父母、及跟自己嚟嘅人入去女仔處、就揸住女仔嘅手對佢話、吠唎吠咕咪、繙譯卽係女仔呀、我咉你起身。個女仔卽時起身、而且曉行因佢係十二歲咯、衆人就了不得、驚奇耶穌嚴禁佢哋、咪俾人知到呢件事、又吩咐俾嘢過女仔食。

第六章

耶穌離開個處番歸自己家鄉、佢嘅門生跟從佢。

2 And when the sabbath day was come, he began to teach in the synagogue: and many hearing *him* were astonished, saying, From whence hath this *man* these things? and what wisdom *is* this which is given unto him, that even such mighty works are wrought by his hands?

3 Is not this the carpenter, the son of Mary, the brother of James, and Joses, and of Juda, and Simon? and are not his sisters here with us? And they were offended at him.

4 But Jesus said unto them, A prophet is not without honour, but in his own country, and among his own kin, and in his own house.

5 And he could there do no mighty work, save that he laid his hands upon a few sick folk, and healed *them*.

6 And he marvelled because of their unbelief. And he went round about the villages, teaching.

7 ¶ And he called *unto him* the twelve, and began to send them forth by two and two; and gave them power over unclean spirits;

8 And commanded them that they should take nothing for *their* journey, save a staff only; no scrip, no bread, no money in *their* purse:

馬可第六章

二適值安息日佢喺會堂教人、眾人聽聞、就見出奇話呢個人從邊處得到嘅呢、所賜過佢嘅係點樣智慧致有叫奇能喺佢手做出呢。佢唔係嗰個木匠嘅仔、做木匠嘅咩、唔係雅各約西猶大西門嘅兄弟咩、佢姊妹唔係同我鄰舍咩、噉就厭棄佢。但耶穌對佢哋話凡係先知除嘵佢家鄉親戚家人之外、無不尊敬佢嘅。耶穌喺個處唔做得乜嘢奇能、不過俾手摩吓幾個病人醫好佢哋咋、而且怪個的人唔信、就周圍去各鄉教人。○耶穌叫個十二個門生、就打發佢哋一對對去賜佢哋有權能趕逐邪鬼。叉吩咐佢哋抆拐杖之外、唔使帶路費或糧食或細袋或擠銀落腰帶。

ST. MARK.

9 But be shod with sandals; and not put on two coats.
10 And he said unto them, In what place soever ye enter into a house, there abide till ye depart from that place.
11 And whosoever shall not receive you, nor hear you, when ye depart thence, shake off the dust under your feet for a testimony against them. Verily I say unto you, It shall be more tolerable for Sodom and Gomorrah in the day of judgment, than for that city.
12 And they went out, and preached that men should repent.
13 And they cast out many devils, and anointed with oil many that were sick, and healed *them*.
14 And king Herod heard *of him*; (for his name was spread abroad;) and he said, That John the Baptist was risen from the dead, and therefore mighty works do shew forth themselves in him.
15 Others said, That it is Elias. And others said, That it is a prophet, or as one of the prophets.
16 But when Herod heard *thereof*, he said, It is John, whom I beheaded: he is risen from the dead.
17 For Herod himself had sent forth and laid hold upon John, and bound him in prison for Herodias' sake, his brother Philip's wife; for he had married her.

獨係着對草鞋、又唔使着兩件衫、又對佢哋話唔論邊處入到人家、就喺個處住、住到你去別處、如有唔接你、唔聽你嘅、臨去之時、你拍曉腳下的塵嚟做佢哋嘅證據。佢生就出去傳道、勸人悔改、又趕逐好多鬼、搣油搽好多病人嚟醫好佢。○耶穌嘅名聲、傳揚起嚟、希律王聽聞就話、佢係施洗禮嘅約翰、由死復生、故此佢做得出大奇能呀、有人話佢係以利亞、又有人話佢係先知、好似古先知中之一、惟係希律聽聞就話呢個係我所斬嘅約翰、佢復生嘞、個個希律也曾使人捉約翰困入監嚟、因佢兄弟腓力嘅妻希羅底緣故、希律已經娶佢咯。

18 For John had said unto Herod, It is not lawful for thee to have thy brother's wife.

19 Therefore Herodias had a quarrel against him, and would have killed him; but she could not :

20 For Herod feared John, knowing that he was a just man and a holy, and observed him; and when he heard him, he did many things, and heard him gladly.

21 And when a convenient day was come, that Herod on his birthday made a supper to his lords, high captains, and chief *estates* of Galilee;

22 And when the daughter of the said Herodias came in, and danced, and pleased Herod and them that sat with him, the king said unto the damsel, Ask of me whatsoever thou wilt, and I will give *it* thee.

23 And he sware unto her, Whatsoever thou shalt ask of me, I will give *it* thee, unto the half of my kingdom.

24 And she went forth, and said unto her mother, What shall I ask? And she said, The head of John the Baptist.

25 And she came in straightway with haste unto the king, and asked, saying, I will that thou give me by and by in a charger the head of John the Baptist.

約翰曾諫希律話你娶兄弟嘅妻係唔合呀。故此希羅底怨恨佢、好想殺佢、但唔殺得。因爲希律知約翰係公義而且聖潔、就敬畏保護佢、聽佢所講多係依住嘅做、又歡喜聽佢講。啱啱有個機會、卽係希律嘅生日、擺設晚席、請各位文武官員與及加利利尊貴嘅人。個希羅底嘅女入去跳舞、令希律及同席嘅人、個個都歡喜。王就對個女話任從你所想嘅嚟求我、我是必俾過你。而且對佢誓願話、但凡你求我嘅雖係要我國一半、我必俾你。個女就出去問佢老母話我應該求乜嘢呢。老母話施洗禮約翰嘅頭喇。個女就趕快入去見王求話我想你揻施洗禮約翰嘅頭、載落盤上、卽時賜我。

ST. MARK.

26 And the king was exceedingly sorry; *yet* for his oath's sake, and for their sakes which sat with him, he would not reject her.

27 And immediately the king sent an executioner, and commanded his head to be brought: and he went and beheaded him in the prison,

28 And brought his head in a charger, and gave it to the damsel; and the damsel gave it to her mother.

29 And when his disciples heard *of it*, they came and took up his corpse, and laid it in a tomb.

30 And the apostles gathered themselves together unto Jesus, and told him all things, both what they had done, and what they had taught.

31 And he said unto them, Come ye yourselves into a desert place, and rest a while: for there were many coming and going, and they had no leisure so much as to eat.

32 And they departed into a desert place by ship privately.

33 And the people saw them departing, and many knew him, and ran afoot thither out of all cities, and outwent them, and came together unto him.

王好閉翳、但因爲已經誓願、又因同席嘅人喺處、唔肯推辭佢。王郎時打發一個兵卒、吩咐佢攞約翰嘅頭、個兵卒就去喺監裏斬曉約翰擰佢個頭落盤摀嚟俾過個女、個女轉交過老母佢嘅門生聽聞、就嚟執拾佢屍葬落墳墓。○使徒聚埋嚟耶穌處、搣所做嘅事所敎嘅道、講嚟佢聽、耶穌對佢哋話、你哋去到曠野幽靜之處、歇息一吓啦、因爲來往嘅人多、令佢食飯都唔得閒。噉就坐船去到曠野幽靜之處、衆人睇見佢哋去好多認得耶穌、就喺各城路上走起、先到佢所去個處

馬可第六章

耶穌出去、睇見羣衆、就可憐佢哋、因佢好似羊咩冇牧人噉、就搣好多道理教佢。到挨晚時佢門生對耶穌話、呢處係曠野、如今挨晚咯、請散衆人等佢去四便鄉村自己買嘢食喇。耶穌答門生話、你俾野佢哋食囉。門生對佢話、我哋搣二十兩銀去買餅俾佢哋食咩。耶穌對門生話、你有幾多餅呢、你去睇吓門生睇過就話有五個餅、共兩條魚呢。耶穌吩咐門生令大衆一隊一隊、坐在草面衆人就坐落或一百一隊、或五十一隊。耶穌摔起個五個餅兩條魚、望住天感謝、擘開的餅俾過門生、令佢擺開衆人面前、又搣兩條魚分俾衆人。

34 And Jesus, when he came out, saw much people, and was moved with compassion toward them, because they were as sheep not having a shepherd: and he began to teach them many things.

35 And when the day was now far spent, his disciples came unto him, and said, This is a desert place, and now the time is far passed:

36 Send them away, that they may go into the country round about, and into the villages, and buy themselves bread: for they have nothing to eat.

37 He answered and said unto them, Give ye them to eat. And they say unto him, Shall we go and buy two hundred pennyworth of bread, and give them to eat?

38 He saith unto them, How many loaves have ye? go and see. And when they knew, they say, Five, and two fishes.

39 And he commanded them to make all sit down by companies upon the green grass.

40 And they sat down in ranks, by hundreds, and by fifties.

41 And when he had taken the five loaves and the two fishes, he looked up to heaven, and blessed, and brake the loaves, and gave *them* to his disciples to set before them; and the two fishes divided he among them all.

St. Mark.

42 And they did all eat, and were filled.
43 And they took up twelve baskets full of the fragments, and of the fishes.
44 And they that did eat of the loaves were about five thousand men.
45 And straightway he constrained his disciples to get into the ship, and to go to the other side before unto Bethsaida, while he sent away the people.
46 And when he had sent them away, he departed into a mountain to pray.
47 And when even was come, the ship was in the midst of the sea, and he alone on the land.
48 And he saw them toiling in rowing; for the wind was contrary unto them: and about the fourth watch of the night he cometh unto them, walking upon the sea, and would have passed by them.
49 But when they saw him walking upon the sea, they supposed it had been a spirit, and cried out:
50 For they all saw him, and were troubled. And immediately he talked with them, and saith unto them, Be of good cheer: it is I; be not afraid.
51 And he went up unto them into the ship; and the wind ceased: and they were sore amazed in themselves beyond measure, and wondered.

嗜就大衆都食飽、就起個的餅碎、及食剩嘅魚足滿十二籃。共計食嘅有五千人。○耶穌就催佢門生落船先過個便岸、到伯賽大等待自己散曉衆人之後、上山祈禱。到夜晚、個隻船喺海中耶穌獨自己喺岸上睇見門生掉槳好辛苦、因爲碰風呀、個晚約嗖到四更時候、耶穌步行海面㗎、到佢哋處好似想經過嘅一樣、門生見佢喺海面行、估係怪物、就叫喊起嚟。因爲人人都見佢、故此咁慌、耶穌卽時對佢哋講話、你哋放心囉、係我呀、唔使怕嗜。就佢上船、到佢哋處、風就息曉、佢哋心中好慌。

52 For they considered not *the miracle* of the loaves; for their heart was hardened.

53 And when they had passed over, they came into the land of Gennesaret, and drew to the shore.

54 And when they were come out of the ship, straightway they knew him,

55 And ran through that whole region round about, and began to carry about in beds those that were sick, where they heard he was.

56 And whithersoever he entered, into villages, or cities, or country, they laid the sick in the streets, and besought him that they might touch if it were but the border of his garment: and as many as touched him were made whole.

CHAPTER 7.

THEN came together unto him the Pharisees, and certain of the scribes, which came from Jerusalem.

2 And when they saw some of his disciples eat bread with defiled, that is to say, with unwashen hands, they found fault.

3 For the Pharisees, and all the Jews, except they wash *their* hands oft, eat not, holding the tradition of the elders.

因爲佢哋心硬唔曉得擘餅嘅異蹟呀。○巴經過海去到革尼撒勒地方、就灣泊岸邊佢哋離船上岸衆人卽時認得佢、走勻四圍地方聞得耶穌喺邊處、就搣牀擡住病人去個處、但凡耶穌所到嘅地方、或係村裏或係城中或係鄉間、人哋擡病人擠倒街上求耶穌俾佢哋摩吓衫邊呞、凡係摩親佢嘅個個就得好番。

第七章。

有啲唎嚷人及幾個讀書人、從耶路撒冷嚟嘅、聚埋耶穌處。見佢幾個門生、手唔潔淨、卽係未曾洗過手就食飯因爲哋唎嚷人及猶太衆人守古人傳落嘅規矩若唔子細洗手就唔食飯。

ST. MARK.

4 And *when they come* from the market, except they wash, they eat not. And many other things there be, which they have received to hold, *as* the washing of cups, and pots, brazen vessels, and of tables.

5 Then the Pharisees and scribes asked him, Why walk not thy disciples according to the tradition of the elders, but eat bread with unwashen hands?

6 He answered and said unto them, Well hath Esaias prophesied of you hypocrites, as it is written, This people honoureth me with *their* lips, but their heart is far from me.

7 Howbeit in vain do they worship me, teaching *for* doctrines the commandments of men.

8 For laying aside the commandment of God, ye hold the tradition of men, *as* the washing of pots and cups: and many other such like things ye do.

9 And he said unto them, Full well ye reject the commandment of God, that ye may keep your own tradition.

10 For Moses said, Honour thy father and thy mother; and, Whoso curseth father or mother, let him die the death:

馬可第七章

又喺市上番嚟、若唔洗亦唔食、重有好多樣佢哋遵守嘅、卽係杯碗銅器及牀都要洗嘅就嘞啦﹑噲人及讀書人問耶穌話你嘅門生做乜唔依古人傳落嘅規矩、手唔潔淨就食飯呢、耶穌答佢哋話以賽亞預先講及你哋僞善嘅係咯、好似聖書有寫呢的百姓祇口恭敬我、但佢個心離我好遠、佢哋祇人所吩咐嘅、作爲道理嚟敎人嘅、佢拜我係徒然呢﹒你哋丢棄 神嘅誡命、執守古人所傳落嘅﹒耶穌又對佢哋話、你哋眞係丢棄 神嘅誡命嚟守自己所傳落嘅咯﹒因摩西有話、要敬你嘅父母、又話、若毀謗父母嘅人必要定死罪。

ST. MARK.

11 But ye say, If a man shall say to his father or mother, *It is* Corban, that is to say, a gift, by whatsoever thou mightest be profited by me; *he shall be free.*

12 And ye suffer him no more to do aught for his father or his mother;

13 Making the word of God of none effect through your tradition, which ye have delivered: and many such like things do ye.

14 ¶ And when he had called all the people *unto him,* he said unto them, Hearken unto me every one *of you,* and understand:

15 There is nothing from without a man, that entering into him can defile him: but the things which come out of him, those are they that defile the man.

16 If any man have ears to hear, let him hear.

17 And when he was entered into the house from the people, his disciples asked him concerning the parable.

18 And he saith unto them, Are ye so without understanding also? Do ye not perceive, that whatsoever thing from without entereth into the man, *it* cannot defile him;

19 Because it entereth not into his heart, but into the belly,' and goeth out into the draught, purging all meats?

馬可第七章

十一 惟係你哋嚟話、若對父母講、我所應當敬奉你嘅物件、做嘵咯噃、卽係做祭物、自

十二 後你哋就唔准佢奉養父母嘅樣、

十三 你哋所做嘅事重有好多係嘅樣、耶穌就叫衆百姓嚟話你哋衆人要聽我講而且

十四 要明白呀。凡喺外便入嘅、不能汚穢人、獨係喺裏便出嘅、致喧汚穢人呃。但凡有耳

十五 可聽嘅、就要聽罅。○耶穌離開衆人入屋、門生將呢個譬喻問佢。耶穌就對佢哋話、

十六 你哋都唔明白咩、豈唔知到凡喺外便入嘅、不能汚穢人、因爲唔係入佢嘅心、乃係

十七 入佢嘅肚、於是遺落厠坑、佢嘅話當作各樣食物係潔淨咯。

ST. MARK.

20 And he said, That which cometh out of the man, that defileth the man.
21 For from within, out of the heart of man, proceed evil thoughts, adulteries, fornications, murders,
22 Thefts, covetousness, wickedness, deceit, lasciviousness, an evil eye, blasphemy, pride, foolishness:
23 All these evil things come from within, and defile the man.
24 ¶ And from thence he arose, and went into the borders of Tyre and Sidon, and entered into a house, and would have no man know *it*: but he could not be hid.
25 For a *certain* woman, whose young daughter had an unclean spirit, heard of him, and came and fell at his feet:
26 The woman was a Greek, a Syrophenician by nation; and she besought him that he would cast forth the devil out of her daughter.
27 But Jesus said unto her, Let the children first be filled: for it is not meet to take the children's bread, and to cast *it* unto the dogs.
28 And she answered and said unto him, Yes, Lord: yet the dogs under the table eat of the children's crumbs.
29 And he said unto her, For this saying go thy way; the devil is gone out of thy daughter.

二十叉話、係人裏頭出嘅、致喧污穢人。因為從裏頭、卽係從人心中所出、有惡念、私通偷嘅、殺人姦淫貪婪惡毒詭譎奢侈妒忌褻瀆驕傲狂妄呢的各樣惡事皆從心裏頭出、整污穢人嘅呀。○耶穌喺個處起行去到推羅西頓交界嘅地方入一間屋想唔俾人知但唔闊得埋適值有一個女人佢嘅女仔被邪鬼所迷聞得耶穌嘅事嚟嘆倒佢脚下呢個女人係希利尼嘅、希利尼或作異邦屬叙利非尼基族佢求耶穌趕逐邪鬼離開佢女。但耶穌對佢話由得仔女先食飽若撦仔女嘅餅搋過狗食唔好呀。女人答佢話主呀、係略但狗在檯下亦得食仔女跌落嘅咋碎吗。耶穌對佢話因呢一句説話、你可以番去、個鬼已經離開你女略。

St. MARK.

30 And when she was come to her house, she found the devil gone out, and her daughter laid upon the bed.

31 ¶ And again, departing from the coasts of Tyre and Sidon, he came unto the sea of Galilee, through the midst of the coasts of Decapolis.

32 And they bring unto him one that was deaf, and had an impediment in his speech; and they beseech him to put his hand upon him.

33 And he took him aside from the multitude, and put his fingers into his ears, and he spit, and touched his tongue;

34 And looking up to heaven, he sighed, and saith unto him, Ephphatha, that is, Be opened.

35 And straightway his ears were opened, and the string of his tongue was loosed, and he spake plain.

36 And he charged them that they should tell no man: but the more he charged them, so much the more a great deal they published *it*;

37 And were beyond measure astonished, saying, He hath done all things well: he maketh both the deaf to hear, and the dumb to speak.

馬可第七章

三十女人番到佢屋跂、見鬼已經出佢、女瞓在床上。○耶穌又離開推羅境界、經過西頓、及低加波利地方、到加利利海邊、有人帶一個耳聾及孻脷嘅人嚟、求耶穌俾手按吓佢。耶穌帶佢離開衆人、搣手指探入佢對耳、唾口水點吓佢條脷、望住天歎一聲、對佢話呌哒咈、繙譯卽係開通嘅解。佢耳就開通脷結解用講得好明白。耶穌禁戒佢哋唔好話人知但越發禁戒佢哋越發傳開衆人了不得叫驚奇就話佢所做嘅事、件件都好佢使聾嘅聽啞嘅講呀。

CHAPTER 8.

IN those days the multitude being very great, and having nothing to eat, Jesus called his disciples *unto him*, and saith unto them,

2 I have compassion on the multitude, because they have now been with me three days, and have nothing to eat:

3 And if I send them away fasting to their own houses, they will faint by the way: for divers of them came from far.

4 And his disciples answered him, From whence can a man satisfy these *men* with bread here in the wilderness?

5 And he asked them, how many loaves have ye? And they said, Seven.

6 And he commanded the people to sit down on the ground: and he took the seven loaves, and gave thanks, and brake, and gave to his disciples to set before *them*; and they did set *them* before the people.

7 And they had a few small fishes: and he blessed, and commanded to set them also before *them*.

8 So they did eat, and were filled: and they took up of the broken *meat* that was left seven baskets.

第八章

當個時又有羣衆聚集、都冇嘢食、耶穌叫佢門生嚟、對佢哋話、我可憐呢的衆人、因佢同我喺處已經三日、如今冇得食、倘若我使佢哋肚餓去歸、喺路上必定發瘡、因為有的係遠處嚟嘅。門生答佢話、喺呢曠野人從邊處得餅嚟、令佢哋食飽呢、耶穌問佢哋話、你哋有幾多餅呢、佢話七個、耶穌吩咐衆人坐落地上、就摔七個餅祝謝擘開俾過門生嚟擺開、佢哋就擺在衆人面前、又有幾條小魚、耶穌祝謝叫門生亦擺開嚟、就大衆都食飽、執番餘剩的碎嘅七籃。

9 And they that had eaten were about four thousand: and he sent them away.

10 ¶ And straightway he entered into a ship with his disciples, and came into the part of Dalmanutha.

11 And the Pharisees came forth, and began to question with him, seeking of him a sign from heaven, tempting him.

12 And he sighed deeply in his spirit, and saith, Why doth this generation seek after a sign? verily I say unto you, There shall no sign be given unto this generation.

13 And he left them, and entering into the ship again departed to the other side.

14 ¶ Now *the disciples* had forgotten to take bread, neither had they in the ship with them more than one loaf.

15 And he charged them, saying, Take heed, beware of the leaven of the Pharisees, and *of* the leaven of Herod.

16 And they reasoned among themselves, saying, *It is* because we have no bread?

17 And when Jesus knew *it*, he saith unto them, Why reason ye, because ye have no bread? perceive ye not yet, neither understand? have ye your heart yet hardened?

18 Having eyes, see ye not? and having ears, hear ye not? and do ye not remember?

⁹個的人大約有四千耶穌就散曉衆人。○即時共佢門生落船去到大馬努大地方。¹¹唎嚁人出嚟盤問耶穌求佢顯出天嚟嘅異蹟係想試佢呀耶穌心中歎息話呢個世代因何求異蹟呢我實在話你知斷唔撒異蹟俾過呢過世代呢。嚟就離開佢哋再落船過對面岸。○門生唔記得帶餅船上獨係有一個餅吥。耶穌做戒佢哋話謹慎提防啲唎嚁人嘅酵種及希律嘅酵種呀門生彼此議論話係因我哋冇餅咻。耶穌知到就對佢哋話做乜搣冇餅嚟議論呢你哋重唔知到唔明白咩你心吶硬睰你有眼唔喺睇有耳唔喺聽亦唔記得咩。

ST. MARK.

19 When I brake the five loaves among five thousand, how many baskets full of fragments took ye up? They say unto him, Twelve.

20 And when the seven among four thousand, how many baskets full of fragments took ye up? And they said, Seven.

21 And he said unto them, How is it that ye do not understand?

22 ¶ And he cometh to Bethsaida; and they bring a blind man unto him, and besought him to touch him.

23 And he took the blind man by the hand, and led him out of the town; and when he had spit on his eyes, and put his hands upon him, he asked him if he saw aught.

24 And he looked up, and said, I see men as trees, walking.

25 After that he put *his* hands again upon his eyes, and made him look up; and he was restored, and saw every man clearly.

26 And he sent him away to his house, saying, Neither go into the town, nor tell *it* to any in the town.

27 ¶ And Jesus went out, and his disciples, into the towns of Cesarea Philippi: and by the way he asked his disciples, saying unto them, Whom do men say that I am?

我擘開五個餅分過五千人食、你執起個的碎嘅、裝滿幾多籃呢。答話、十二籃。又擘開七個餅分過四千人食、你執起個的碎嘅、裝滿幾多籃呢。答話、七籃。就對佢他話、你他重唔明白咩。○佢他到曉伯賽大、有人帶一個盲眼嘅人埋、求耶穌摩佢。耶穌揸住盲眼人嘅手帶佢出去村外、俾口水唾佢雙眼、又搣對手按吓佢、問佢你見嘢唔見呢。盲眼嘅舉頭一望、就話我睇見人行好似樹㗎樣、後來再搣手按吓佢對眼、令佢定眼望吓、就好嘅、各樣睇得明白。耶穌打發佢歸家話、個條村你都唔好入去、亦唔好話村人他話我係也誰呢。○耶穌共門生去到該撒利亞腓立比各村、喺路上問佢門生話人他話我係也

28 And they answered, John the Baptist: but some *say*, Elias; and others, One of the prophets.

29 And he saith unto them, But whom say ye that I am? And Peter answereth and saith unto him, Thou art the Christ.

30 And he charged them that they should tell no man of him.

31 And he began to teach them, that the Son of Man must suffer many things, and be rejected of the elders, and *of* the chief priests, and scribes, and be killed, and after three days rise again.

32 And he spake that saying openly. And Peter took him, and began to rebuke him.

33 But when he had turned about and looked on his disciples, he rebuked Peter, saying, Get thee behind me, Satan: for thou savourest not the things that be of God, but the things that be of men.

34 ¶ And when he had called the people *unto him* with his disciples also, he said unto them, Whosoever will come after me, let him deny himself, and take up his cross, and follow me.

35 For whosoever will save his life shall lose it; but whosoever shall lose his life for my sake and the gospel's, the same shall save it.

36 For what shall it profit a man, if he shall gain the whole world, and lose his own soul?

佢哋答話、有的話係施洗禮嘅約翰、有的話係先知中之一。耶穌又問佢哋話、但你哋話我係也誰呢、彼得答話你係基督路耶穌禁戒佢哋、唔好講佢嘅事過人知。又起首教訓佢哋話人子必受好多害、彼個的長老共眾祭司長、及讀書人丟棄而且被人殺過三日就復生佢話白呢的說話、彼得就拉埋佢嚟勸諫耶穌回頭望住門生、責彼得話撒但退囉、你唔係體貼神嘅情、乃係體貼人嘅情呃。就叫眾人及門生嚟對佢哋話、人若想跟從我嘅、必要克勝自己貯住佢十字架嚟跟我。因為但凡想救自己生命嘅、必定失佢生命、但凡為我及福音失曉佢生命嘅、必定救番佢生命人若得哓普天下而失曉佢生命、或日生命當作靈魂、有乜益呢。

ST. MARK.

37 Or what shall a man give in exchange for his soul?

38 Whosoever therefore shall be ashamed of me and of my words, in this adulterous and sinful generation, of him also shall the Son of man be ashamed, when he cometh in the glory of his Father with the holy angels.

CHAPTER 9.

AND he said unto them, Verily I say unto you, That there be some of them that stand here, which shall not taste of death, till they have seen the kingdom of God come with power.

2 ¶ And after six days Jesus taketh *with him* Peter, and James, and John, and leadeth them up into a high mountain apart by themselves: and he was transfigured before them.

3 And his raiment became shining, exceeding white as snow; so as no fuller on earth can white them.

4 And there appeared unto them Elias with Moses: and they were talking with Jesus.

5 And Peter answered and said to Jesus, Master, it is good for us to be here: and let us make three tabernacles; one for thee, and one for Moses, and one for Elias.

馬可第九章

人嗑拡乜嘢嚟贖番佢生命呢。但凡喺呢個姦惡世代當我共我嘅道理係羞恥到人子乘天父榮光共埋聖使降臨個時佢亦必當個個人係羞恥略。

第九章

耶穌又對佢哋話、我實在話你知、企倒呢處嘅、有的人未死之死、必得見 神國、好有權柄臨到嘅。○過六日耶穌帶住彼得雅各約翰、同埋上高山幽靜之處、喺佢哋面前變化佢嘅衣服光明、色水極白世上漂布嘅人、都唔漂得叫白個時佢哋又見以利亞摩西現出嚟共耶穌講彼得對耶穌話夫子、我哋喺呢處好略、等我搭三間茅屋、一間爲你、一間爲摩西一間爲以利亞。

40 ST. MARK.

6 For he wist not what to say; for they were sore afraid.

7 And there was a cloud that overshadowed them: and a voice came out of the cloud, saying, This is my beloved Son: hear him.

8 And suddenly, when they had looked round about, they saw no man any more, save Jesus only with themselves.

9 And as they came down from the mountain, he charged them that they should tell no man what things they had seen, till the Son of man were risen from the dead.

10 And they kept that saying with themselves, questioning one with another what the rising from the dead should mean.

11 And they asked him, saying, Why say the scribes that Elias must first come?

12 And he answered and told them, Elias verily cometh first, and restoreth all things; and how it is written of the Son of man, that he must suffer many things, and be set at nought.

13 But I say unto you, That Elias is indeed come, and they have done unto him whatsoever they listed, as it is written of him.

14 ¶ And when he came to *his* disciples, he saw a great multitude about them, and the scribes questioning with them.

馬可第九章

六佢唔知自己講乜嘢、因爲三個門生都好慌呀。適值有雲遮住佢哋、有聲喺雲中出嚟話、呢個係我嘅愛子、你哋要聽佢話呀。門生忽然周圍望吓、一個人都唔見獨係耶穌共自己喺處㖃。○落山個時耶穌禁戒佢哋話人子未曾由死復生、係乜嘢意思。又問耶穌話爲乜事讀書人話以利亞必要先嚟呢。耶穌對佢哋話以利亞真係先嚟、再與起各樣嘅事、而且聖經論及人子點話佢必定受好多害、被人輕忽呢。但我話你哋知以利亞已經嚟、衆人隨意待佢、照依聖經所講及佢嘅咯。○耶穌到門生處見大多人圍住佢哋、又有讀書人共佢哋辯論。

ST. MARK.

15 And straightway all the people, when they beheld him, were greatly amazed, and running to him saluted him.

16 And he asked the scribes, What question ye with them?

17 And one of the multitude answered and said, Master, I have brought unto thee my son, which hath a dumb spirit;

18 And wheresoever he taketh him, he teareth him; and he foameth, and gnasheth with his teeth, and pineth away: and I spake to thy disciples that they should cast him out; and they could not.

19 He answereth him, and saith, O faithless generation, how long shall I be with you? how long shall I suffer you? bring him unto me.

20 And they brought him unto him: and when he saw him, straightway the spirit tare him; and he fell on the ground, and wallowed foaming.

21 And he asked his father, How long is it ago since this came unto him? And he said, Of a child.

22 And ofttimes it hath cast him into the fire, and into the waters, to destroy him: but if thou canst do any thing, have compassion on us, and help us.

23 Jesus said unto him, If thou canst believe, all things *are* possible to him that believeth.

大眾一見耶穌、十分驚異、走前去問佢安。耶穌就問個的讀書人話、你共佢辯論乜嘢呢。眾人之中有一個答佢話、老師、我帶我嘅仔嚟你處、佢係被啞鬼所迷嘅唔論喺邊處搖佢、就令佢跌倒流口水咬牙乾瘦咯、我也曾請你門生趕佢、但佢哋不能耶穌答佢話、唉冇信德嘅世代呀、我同你喺得處幾耐我忍耐得你幾耐呢、帶個仔嚟我處喇、佢哋就帶佢嚟、一見耶穌、鬼就縮攣佢、撲倒地處、翻來覆去兼流口水。耶穌問佢父親、你仔得嚟嘅病幾耐呢、佢話自細時係噉咯。個鬼屢次揼佢落水火之中、想滅曉佢、倘若你能做得嚟、就憐憫幫助我哋咯。耶穌對佢話、你使乜講倘若你能個句說話呢、有信嘅人、樣樣都做得呀。

24 And straightway the father of the child cried out, and said with tears, Lord, I believe; help thou mine unbelief.

25 When Jesus saw that the people came running together, he rebuked the foul spirit, saying unto him, Thou dumb and deaf spirit, I charge thee, come out of him, and enter no more into him.

26 And *the spirit* cried, and rent him sore, and came out of him: and he was as one dead; insomuch that many said, He is dead.

27 But Jesus took him by the hand, and lifted him up; and he arose.

28 And when he was come into the house, his disciples asked him privately, Why could not we cast him out?

29 And he said unto them, This kind can come forth by nothing, but by prayer and fasting.

30 ¶ And they departed thence, and passed through Galilee; and he would not that any man should know *it*.

31 For he taught his disciples, and said unto them, The Son of man is delivered into the hands of men, and they shall kill him; and after that he is killed, he shall rise the third day.

32 But they understood not that saying, and were afraid to ask him.

個仔嘅父親、卽時流眼淚大聲叫話、我信、但我信不足、求你幫助喇。耶穌見衆人走埋佢處、就責罰個邪鬼話聾啞嘅鬼呀、我吩咐你喺佢處出嚟、又咪番入去、嗰個鬼就大聲叫、縮攣佢好辛苦、就出去、個仔好似死一樣、至到衆人都話佢死曉咯。但耶穌執住佢手拖佢起、佢就起身。耶穌入屋門生靜靜問佢話、我哋做乜唔趕得佢出呢。耶穌對佢哋話、倘若祈禱禁食呢的族類唔出去嚟。○嚟佢哋就離開個處、經過加利利耶穌唔想人知到因教佢門生話人子必要賣過人手、人哋是必殺佢、被殺之後第三日復生門生唔明白呢句說話、又唔敢問佢。

ST. MARK.

33 ¶ And he came to Capernaum: and being in the house he asked them, What was it that ye disputed among yourselves by the way?

34 But they held their peace: for by the way they had disputed among themselves, who *should be* the greatest.

35 And he sat down, and called the twelve, and saith unto them, If any man desire to be first, *the same* shall be last of all, and servant of all.

36 And he took a child, and set him in the midst of them: and when he had taken him in his arms, he said unto them,

37 Whosoever shall receive one of such children in my name, receiveth me; and whosoever shall receive me, receiveth not me, but him that sent me.

38 ¶ And John answered him, saying, Master, we saw one casting out devils in thy name, and he followeth not us; and we forbade him, because he followeth not us.

39 But Jesus said, Forbid him not: for there is no man which shall do a miracle in my name, that can lightly speak evil of me.

40 For he that is not against us is on our part.

○大衆到曉迦百農、在屋內耶穌問門生話、你哋喺路上議論乜嘢呢。門生唔出聲、因爲喺路上爭論乜誰係做至大呀。耶穌坐處、叫個十二個門生嚟對佢話、有人想做先頭嘅、是必做衆人嘅尾後、做衆人嘅使喚人。耶穌就帶一個細仔嚟、擠倒衆人中間、又抱起佢、對門生話、但凡托我名、接納一個噉樣嘅細仔、卽係接納我、但凡接納我嘅、卽係接納打發我嚟個位呀。○約翰對耶穌話、老師我哋見一個人、托你名嚟趕鬼我哋、就禁止佢、因佢跟從我哋嘅。耶穌話唔好禁止佢、因爲未有人托我名嚟做異蹟、倒轉輕易毀謗我嘅。但凡唔共我哋做對敵嘅、就係歸從我哋嘅咯。

ST. MARK.

41 For whosoever shall give you a cup of water to drink in my name, because ye belong to Christ, verily I say unto you, he shall not lose his reward.

42 And whosoever shall offend one of *these* little ones that believe in me, it is better for him that a millstone were hanged about his neck, and he were cast into the sea.

43 And if thy hand offend thee, cut it off; it is better for thee to enter into life maimed, than having two hands to go into hell, into the fire that never shall be quenched:

44 Where their worm dieth not, and the fire is not quenched.

45 And if thy foot offend thee, cut it off: it is better for thee to enter halt into life, than having two feet to be cast into hell, into the fire that never shall be quenched:

46 Where their worm dieth not, and the fire is not quenched.

47 And if thine eye offend thee, pluck it out: it is better for thee to enter into the kingdom of God with one eye, than having two eyes to be cast into hell fire:

48 Where their worm dieth not, and the fire is not quenched.

馬可第九章

但凡搣一杯水俾你哋飲、因你係屬基督嘅我實在話你知、個人必定唔失佢嘅賞賜咯。但凡令一個信我之小子陷罪嘅、佢불可被大石磨掛住頸、拪落海重好呀。倘若一隻手陷你犯罪、就斬斷佢、你跛手入永生、重好過有兩隻手落火不熄嘅地獄。倘若一隻脚陷你犯罪、就斬斷佢、你跛脚入永生、重好過有兩隻脚落地獄。倘若一隻眼陷你犯罪、就挖曉佢、你單眼入神國、重好過有兩隻眼落地獄嘅。個處虫唔死、火唔熄嘅。

ST. MARK.

49 For every one shall be salted with fire, and every sacrifice shall be salted with salt.

50 Salt *is* good: but if the salt have lost his saltness, wherewith will ye season it? Have salt in yourselves, and have peace one with another.

CHAPTER 10.

AND he arose from thence, and cometh into the coasts of Judea by the farther side of Jordan: and the people resort unto him again; and, as he was wont, he taught them again.

2 ¶ And the Pharisees came to him, and asked him, Is it lawful for a man to put away *his* wife? tempting him.

3 And he answered and said unto them, What did Moses command you?

4 And they said, Moses suffered to write a bill of divorcement, and to put *her* away.

5 And Jesus answered and said unto them, For the hardness of your heart he wrote you this precept.

6 But from the beginning of the creation God made them male and female.

7 For this cause shall a man leave his father and mother, and cleave to his wife;

因為凡人必用火嚟煉佢、凡祭物必用鹽落去。鹽係好嘅、倘若鹽失曉味、點得番鹹呢、你哋裏頭應該有鹽彼此調和呀。

第十章

耶穌由個處起行、經過約但河外、到猶太嘅境地、衆人再聚埋嚟佢處、耶穌照常再教佢哋。○啩唎嘅人想試耶穌問佢話、人出妻着唔着呢、耶穌答佢哋話、摩西准我哋寫分書嚟、出佢呀。耶穌答佢哋話、因你哋心硬、故此為你哋寫落呢的誡命佢、起首創造個時、神造出有男有女。故此人將離開父母、共妻膠合、

8 And they twain shall be one flesh: so then they are no more twain, but one flesh.

9 What therefore God hath joined together, let not man put asunder.

10 And in the house his disciples asked him again of the same *matter*.

11 And he saith unto them, Whosoever shall put away his wife, and marry another, committeth adultery against her.

12 And if a woman shall put away her husband, and be married to another, she committeth adultery.

13 ¶ And they brought young children to him, that he should touch them; and *his* disciples rebuked those that brought *them*.

14 But when Jesus saw *it*, he was much displeased, and said unto them, Suffer the little children to come unto me, and forbid them not; for of such is the kingdom of God.

15 Verily I say unto you, Whosoever shall not receive the kingdom of God as a little child, he shall not enter therein.

16 And he took them up in his arms, put *his* hands upon them, and blessed them.

兩人成為一體嚇就唔重算係兩個算係一體呀所以　神所配合嘅人唔好分開、

耶穌喺屋裏門生再搣呢件事嚟問佢耶穌對佢哋話、但凡出佢妻娶過別個嘅就係辜負個妻、嚟犯姦淫罅。倘若妻丟棄丈夫嫁過別人佢亦係犯姦淫罅。○有人帶住的嫩仔嚟、想耶穌摩吓門生責罰佢哋。但耶穌一見就唔歡喜對門生話由得個的嫩仔嚟我處、唔好禁止佢因為得　神國嘅正係嚟樣嘅人呀、我實在話你哋知、但凡承受　神國嘅唔似嫩仔嚟樣必唔入得個國嘅就抱起個的嫩仔俾手按吓佢、祝福佢。

St. MARK.

17 ¶ And when he was gone forth into the way, there came one running, and kneeled to him, and asked him, Good Master, what shall I do that I may inherit eternal life?

18 And Jesus said unto him, Why callest thou me good? *there is* none good but one, *that is,* God.

19 Thou knowest the commandments, Do not commit adultery, Do not kill, Do not steal, Do not bear false witness, Defraud not, Honour thy father and mother.

20 And he answered and said unto him, Master, all these have I observed from my youth.

21 Then Jesus beholding him loved him, and said unto him, One thing thou lackest: go thy way, sell whatsoever thou hast, and give to the poor, and thou shalt have treasure in heaven: and come, take up the cross, and follow me.

22 And he was sad at that saying, and went away grieved: for he had great possessions.

23 ¶ And Jesus looked round about, and saith unto his disciples, How hardly shall they that have riches enter into the kingdom of God!

○耶穌出去路上有一人走到面前跪倒處問佢話良善嘅老師呀、我要做乜嘢、致得永生呢。耶穌對佢話你爲乜稱我良善呢除曉　神之外冇一個係良善嘅。各條誡命你識哩、卽係唔好殺人、唔好行淫、唔好偷嘢、唔好妄證、唔好呃騙人、又要孝敬你嘅父母佢對耶穌話老師呢各條誡我自少時都守住咯。耶穌睇住佢、愛痛佢、就對佢話你重少一件呀、去賣曬你所有嘅、嚟周濟窮人、就是必有財帛喺天上而且嚟跟從我佢聽聞呢啲說話就變曉面色閉翳而去因爲佢有好多產業呀。耶穌周圍望吓、對佢門生話有錢財嘅人入　神國係好難嘅。

24 And the disciples were astonished at his words. But Jesus answereth again, and s ith unto them, Children, how hard is it for them that trust in riches to enter into the kingdom of God!

25 It is easier for a camel to go through the eye of a needle, than for a rich man to enter into the kingdom of God.

26 And they were astonished out of measure, saying among themselves, Who then can be saved?

27 And Jesus looking upon them saith, With men *it is* impossible, but not with God: for with God all things are possible.

28 ¶ Then Peter began to say unto him, Lo, we have left all, and have followed thee.

29 And Jesus answered and said, Verily I say unto you, There is no man that hath left house, or brethren, or sisters, or father, or mother, or wife, or children, or lands, for my sake, and the gospel's,

30 But he shall receive a hundredfold now in this time, houses, and brethren, and sisters, and mothers, and children, and lands, with persecutions; and in the world to come eternal life.

門生驚奇佢嘅說話耶穌再答佢哋話、小子呀、恃錢財嘅人入 神國、係好難略。

駝穿過針眼、比較財主人入 神國更容易呀、門生了不得咁驚奇就對佢話啵就

也誰可以得救呢。耶穌望住佢哋話在人實係不能、在 神就唔係、因爲 神係無

所不能呀。○彼得就對耶穌話、我哋已經捨曉所有嘅㗎跟從你咯、耶穌答話我實

在話你哋知爲我及福音離開屋宇兄弟姊妹父母仔女田地嘅、未有唔喺今世得

番百倍嘅、卽係屋宇兄弟姊妹母親兒女田地亦有迫害、惟係來世得永生。

ST. MARK.

31 But many *that are* first shall be last; and the last first.

32 ¶ And they were in the way going up to Jerusalem; and Jesus went before them: and they were amazed; and as they followed, they were afraid. And he took again the twelve, and began to tell them what things should happen unto him,

33 *Saying,* Behold, we go up to Jerusalem; and the Son of Man shall be delivered unto the chief priests, and unto the scribes; and they shall condemn him to death, and shall deliver him to the Gentiles:

34 And they shall mock him, and shall scourge him, and shall spit upon him, and shall kill him; and the third day he shall rise again.

35 ¶ And James and John, the sons of Zebedee, come unto him, saying, Master, we would that thou shouldest do for us whatsoever we shall desire.

36 And he said unto them, What would ye that I should do for you?

37 They said unto him, Grant unto us that we may sit, one on thy right hand, and the other on thy left hand, in thy glory.

馬可第十章

三一 但好多先頭嘅人、將做尾後尾後嘅人、將做先頭呀。○ 佢哋上耶路撒冷個時喺路上、耶穌先行、門生見好出奇跟從嘅又見驚慌、耶穌再帶住十二門生㧒自己將遇嘅事對佢哋講話我哋上耶路撒冷人子必被人交過衆祭司長及讀書人佢哋將定佢死罪、解過異邦人、又必凌辱佢、俾口水唾佢、鞭打佢、又殺佢、到第三日佢就復生㗎。○ 西比太嘅仔雅各約翰嚟到耶穌處話老師我哋所有求你嘅、想你共我哋做呀。耶穌對佢哋話你想我共你做乜嘢呢佢哋答話你乘榮個時求賜我哋一個坐你右便、一個坐你左便呀。

ST. MARK.

38 But Jesus said unto them, Ye know not what ye ask: can ye drink of the cup that I drink of? and be baptized with the baptism that I am baptized with?

39 And they said unto him, We can. And Jesus said unto them, Ye shall indeed drink of the cup that I drink of; and with the baptism that I am baptized withal shall ye be baptized:

40 But to sit on my right hand and on my left hand is not mine to give; but *it shall be given to them* for whom it is prepared.

41 And when the ten heard *it*, they began to be much displeased with James and John.

42 But Jesus called them *to him*, and saith unto them, Ye know that they which are accounted to rule over the Gentiles exercise lordship over them; and their great ones exercise authority upon them.

43 But so shall it not be among you: but whosoever will be great among you, shall be your minister:

44 And whosoever of you will be the chiefest, shall be servant of all.

45 For even the Son of Man came not to be ministered unto, but to minister, and to give his life a ransom for many.

耶穌對佢哋話、你唔知到你所求嘅路、我所飲嘅杯、你飲得唔呢、我所受嘅洗禮、你受得唔呢。佢哋話做得耶穌對佢話、我所飲嘅杯、你哋是必飲、我所受嘅洗禮、你哋是必受。但坐我左便右便、唔係我賜得、獨係預備賜過乜誰就賜過佢咭。十個門生聽聞、就好唔歡喜雅各約翰耶穌叫佢哋嚟話異邦人嘅君王、做佢哋嘅主、大臣用權柄嚟管理佢哋、呢的你知到哩。惟係你哋唔好嘅樣、你哋之中、也誰想做大嘅、必做你哋嘅使噢人也誰想做頭目嘅、必做衆人嘅奴僕。因爲人子嚟、唔係要人服事佢、乃係佢服事人、而且捨自己生命替衆人贖罪呀。

ST. MARK.

46 ¶ And they came to Jericho: and as he went out of Jericho with his disciples and a great number of people, blind Bartimeus, the son of Timeus, sat by the highway side begging.

47 And when he heard that it was Jesus of Nazareth, he began to cry out, and say, Jesus, *thou* Son of David, have mercy on me.

48 And many charged him that he should hold his peace: but he cried the more a great deal, *Thou* Son of David, have mercy on me.

49 And Jesus stood still, and commanded him to be called. And they call the blind man, saying unto him, Be of good comfort, rise; he calleth thee.

50 And he, casting away his garment, rose, and came to Jesus.

51 And Jesus answered and said unto him, What wilt thou that I should do unto thee? The blind man said unto him, Lord, that I might receive my sight.

52 And Jesus said unto him, Go thy way; thy faith hath made thee whole. And immediately he received his sight, and followed Jesus in the way.

○到曉耶利哥耶穌共門生、及大衆出耶利哥時、有個盲眼乞兒、卽係底買嘅仔巴底買、坐倒路邊開得係拿撒勒耶穌、就大聲叫話、大闢嘅子孫、可憐我呀、衆人責成佢叫佢咪出聲佢越發大聲叫話、大闢嘅子孫、可憐我呀。耶穌歇住脚話叫佢嚟、個的人就叫個盲眼嘅話你安心起身喇耶穌叫你呀。佢就丟棄衣服急的起身、嚟到耶穌處耶穌對佢話你想我共你做乜嘢呢盲眼嘅答話、主呀、我想睇得見呀。耶穌對佢話你去喇你嘅信德醫好你路佢卽時睇得見就喺路上跟從耶穌而去。

CHAPTER II.

AND when they came nigh to Jerusalem, unto Bethphage and Bethany, at the mount of Olives, he sendeth forth two of his disciples,

2 And saith unto them, Go your way into the village over against you: and as soon as ye be entered into it, ye shall find a colt tied, whereon never man sat; loose him, and bring *him*.

3 And if any man say unto you, Why do ye this? say ye that the Lord hath need of him; and straightway he will send him hither.

4 And they went their way, and found the colt tied by the door without in a place where two ways met; and they loose him.

5 And certain of them that stood there said unto them, What do ye, loosing the colt?

6 And they said unto them even as Jesus had commanded: and they let them go.

7 And they brought the colt to Jesus, and cast their garments on him; and he sat upon him.

第十一章

一將近耶路撒冷到伯法其及伯大尼嚟橄欖山處、耶穌打發兩個門生、對佢哋話、你二去對面個條村入到個時、必遇着一隻驢仔綁倒處、歷來未有人騎過嘅、你就解用佢、拉佢嚟。三倘若有人問話你哋解驢做乜嘢、你就話主要用佢呀、個人必卽時俾佢門生就去、果然遇着隻驢仔綁倒門外街邊、就解用佢。五企倒個處嘅、有的人對佢哋話、解個隻驢仔做乜嘢呢、門生照依耶穌所講嘅嚟答佢、個的人就任從佢拉旣七拉驢仔到耶穌處、佢哋搣自己嘅衫鋪落驢背、耶穌騎上去。

ST. MARK.

8 And many spread their garments in the way; and others cut down branches off the trees, and strewed *them* in the way.

9 And they that went before, and they that followed, cried, saying, Hosanna; Blessed *is* he that cometh in the name of the Lord:

10 Blessed *be* the kingdom of our father David, that cometh in the name of the Lord: Hosanna in the highest.

11 And Jesus entered into Jerusalem, and into the temple: and when he had looked round about upon all things, and now the eventide was come, he went out unto Bethany with the twelve.

12 ¶ And on the morrow, when they were come from Bethany, he was hungry:

13 And seeing a fig tree afar off having leaves, he came, if haply he might find any thing thereon: and when he came to it, he found nothing but leaves; for the time of figs was not *yet*.

14 And Jesus answered and said unto it, No man eat fruit of thee hereafter for ever. And his disciples heard *it*.

馬可第十一章

⁸有好多人搣自己衫鋪在路上、亦有人在田斬樹枝鋪在路上。前便行後便跟嘅人大聲叫話萬福呀、應該得福呀、我哋祖宗大闢嘅國將近嚟嘅應得福呀、萬福在至上嘅呀。耶穌到耶路撒冷入去殿堂周圍睇各樣物件、時候已經夜遠、就同十二門生出去、到伯大尼。○第二日佢哋自伯大尼番嚟個時耶穌肚餓、遠遠見無花果樹有葉、就行埋去、想睇佢上頭揾的果子及去到、淨係見葉呮、因為收果嘅時候未到呀。耶穌就對個숭樹話自今以後永遠冇人食你嘅果咯、佢門生都聽見。

15 ¶ And they come to Jerusalem: and Jesus went into the temple, and began to cast out them that sold and bought in the temple, and overthrew the tables of the money changers, and the seats of them that sold doves;

16 And would not suffer that any man should carry any vessel through the temple.

17 And he taught, saying unto them, Is it not written, My house shall be called of all nations the house of prayer? but ye have made it a den of thieves.

18 And the scribes and chief priests heard it, and sought how they might destroy him: for they feared him, because all the people was astonished at his doctrine.

19 And when even was come, he went out of the city.

20 ¶ And in the morning, as they passed by, they saw the fig tree dried up from the roots.

21 And Peter calling to remembrance saith unto him, Master, behold, the fig tree which thou cursedst is withered away.

22 And Jesus answering saith unto them, Have faith in God.

佢哋到曉耶路撒冷耶穌入殿堂就趕個喺殿裏買賣嘅、推倒個的找錢嘅檯、與及賣白鴿的人嘅椅、又唔准人揸器具經過殿裏就教訓佢哋話、聖經唔係有寫、我屋必叫做萬民祈禱嘅屋咩、但你哋減佢嚟做賊巢呀。眾祭司長及讚書人聽聞呢的說話想揾計嚟殺佢但又怕佢因爲眾人驚奇佢嘅教訓呀。○ 到挨晚時耶穌出城去。第二朝佢哋經過見個簷無花果樹連根都乾曉。彼得記起就對佢話夫子請睇吓你所咒詛嘅無花果樹巳經乾枯路。耶穌答佢哋話、你哋當要信 神。

ST. MARK.

23 For verily I say unto you, That whosoever shall say unto this mountain, Be thou removed, and be thou cast into the sea; and shall not doubt in his heart, but shall believe that those things which he saith shall come to pass; he shall have whatsoever he saith.

24 Therefore I say unto you, What things soever ye desire, when ye pray, believe that ye receive *them*, and ye shall have *them*.

25 And when ye stand praying, forgive, if ye have aught against any; that your Father also which is in heaven may forgive you your trespasses.

26 But if ye do not forgive, neither will your Father which is in heaven forgive your trespasses.

27 ¶ And they come again to Jerusalem: and as he was walking in the temple, there come to him the chief priests, and the scribes and the elders,

28 And say unto him, By what authority doest thou these things? and who gave thee this authority to do these things?

29 And Jesus answered and said unto them, I will also ask of you one question, and answer me, and I will tell you by what authority I do these things.

我實在話你知、佢凡對呢個山話、搬去抌落海、如果心中冇思疑信呢句說話必成就、㗎就、一的都成就㗎。故此我話你知當祈禱時若係共人有仇恨、你哋企處祈禱時若唔赦免佢、你父在天亦唔赦免你罪咯。○佢哋再到耶路撒冷、耶穌喺殿間行、衆祭司長、讀書人、及長老嚟到、對佢話你抳乜嘢權柄做呢的事呢、又乜誰賜你呢的權柄、令你做得啲樣呢。耶穌對佢哋話我亦有一句說話問你、請你答我、我就話你知、我抳乜嘢權柄做呢的事略。

ST. MARK.

30 The baptism of John, was *it* from heaven, or of men? answer me.

31 And they reasoned with themselves, saying, If we shall say, From heaven; he will say, Why then did ye not believe him?

32 But if we shall say, Of men; they feared the people: for all *men* counted John, that he was a prophet indeed.

33 And they answered and said unto Jesus, We cannot tell. And Jesus answering saith unto them, Neither do I tell you by what authority I do these things.

CHAPTER 12.

AND he began to speak unto them by parables. A *certain* man planted a vineyard, and set a hedge about *it*, and digged *a place for* the winefat, and built a tower, and let it out to husbandmen, and went into a far country.

2 And at the season he sent to the husbandmen a servant, that he might receive from the husbandmen of the fruit of the vineyard.

3 And they caught *him*, and beat him, and sent *him* away empty.

馬可第十二章

約翰嘅洗禮、係由天嚟嘅呀、抑或由人嚟嘅呢、請你答我、佢哋私下議論話、我哋若話係由天嚟嘅、佢是必問、做乜你哋唔信佢呢、若話係由人嚟嘅、又慌住百姓、因爲衆人以爲約翰眞係先知呀、佢哋就答耶穌話我哋唔知、耶穌對佢話、我亦唔話你哋知我憑也嘢權柄做呢啲事略。

第十二章

耶穌就設譬喻對衆人話、有個人種菩提園、俾籬圍住、掘個酒醡、又起個更樓、租過農夫就去遠處地方、到期打發一個僕去農夫處、想向農夫收園中應納嘅果、農夫捉倒佢嚟打令佢空手番去。

ST. MARK.

4 And again he sent unto them another servant; and at him they cast stones, and wounded *him* in the head, and sent *him* away shamefully handled.

5 And again he sent another; and him they killed, and many others; beating some, and killing some.

6 Having yet therefore one son, his well beloved, he sent him also last unto them, saying, They will reverence my son.

7 But those husbandmen said among themselves, This is the heir; come, let us kill him, and the inheritance shall be ours.

8 And they took him, and killed *him*, and cast *him* out of the vineyard.

9 What shall therefore the lord of the vineyard do? he will come and destroy the husbandmen, and will give the vineyard unto others.

10 And have ye not read this Scripture; The stone which the builders rejected is become the head of the corner:

11 This was the Lord's doing, and it is marvellous in our eyes?

12 And they sought to lay hold on him, but feared the people; for they knew that he had spoken the parable against them: and they left him, and went their way.

再打發第二個僕去、農夫打傷佢頭、令佢羞辱返。
打發好多僕去有的被佢打有的被佢殺。
打發佢去、話佢哋是必恭敬我仔、但個的農夫相講話、呢個係承受家業嘅仔、我哋嚟殺死佢、家業就歸我哋路。於是執住佢殺曉、丟出園外。嗱個園主要點樣做呢、是必嚟滅個的農夫搣個園租過別人路。聖經有寫起屋師傅所丟棄嘅石、做曉屋角第一嚱石。呢的係主所做成嘅、在我哋眼中見出奇咯。呢幾句書、你哋未讀過咩。個的人知到耶穌設譬喻、係指佢哋、所以想捉佢、但係怕眾人、嚟就離開佢去曉。

ST. MARK.

13 ¶ And they send unto him certain of the Pharisees and of the Herodians, to catch him in *his* words.

14 And when they were come, they say unto him, Master, we know that thou art true, and carest for no man; for thou regardest not the person of men, but teachest the way of God in truth: Is it lawful to give tribute to Cesar, or not?

15 Shall we give, or shall we not give? But he, knowing their hypocrisy, said unto them, Why tempt ye me? bring me a penny, that I may see *it*.

16 And they brought *it*. And he saith unto them, Whose *is* this image and superscription? And they said unto him, Cesar's.

17 And Jesus answering said unto them, Render to Cesar the things that are Cesar's, and to God the things that are God's. And they marvelled at him.

18 ¶ Then come unto him the Sadducees, which say there is no resurrection; and they asked him, saying,

19 Master, Moses wrote unto us, If a man's brother die, and leave *his* wife *behind him*, and leave no children, that his brother should take his wife, and raise up seed unto his brother.

○後來、打發啲唎嘩人、及希律黨幾個人嚟、想執佢說話嚟陷害佢、佢哋嚟到、對耶穌話、老師、我哋知你係真實冇偏心待人嘅、因你唔係撠外貌嚟取人、乃係撠真實嚟傳 神嘅道、納稅過該撒着唔着呢、我哋納唔納呢。但耶穌知到佢詐偽、就話做嚟、你哋試我呢、你揸一個銀錢仔俾我睇。佢哋就揸嚟嘅。耶穌對佢哋話呢個相㨃共也、你哋話係邊個嘅。佢哋話係該撒嘅。耶穌對佢哋話該撒嘅物件納過該撒、 神嘅物件納過 神略。眾人就驚奇佢。○又有噠吐嘰人、卽係話人死冇復生嘅嚟問耶穌話、老師摩西嘅書寫落過我哋話、倘若人嘅兄長死曉、剩落個妻冇仔、兄弟要娶佢嘅妻等生仔嚟承繼佢。

St. MARK.

20 Now there were seven brethren: and the first took a wife, and dying left no seed.

21 And the second took her, and died, neither left he any seed: and the third likewise.

22 And the seven had her, and left no seed: last of all the woman died also.

23 In the resurrection therefore, when they shall rise, whose wife shall she be of them? for the seven had her to wife.

24 And Jesus answering said unto them, Do ye not therefore err, because ye know not the Scriptures, neither the power of God?

25 For when they shall rise from the dead, they neither marry, nor are given in marriage; but are as the angels which are in heaven.

26 And as touching the dead, that they rise; have ye not read in the book of Moses, how in the bush God spake unto him, saying, I *am* the God of Abraham, and the God of Isaac, and the God of Jacob?

27 He is not the God of the dead, but the God of the living: ye therefore do greatly err.

從前有七個兄弟、至大嘅娶妻冇仔留落死曉、第二嘅娶佢、亦係冇仔留落死曉、第三嘅亦係噉樣。七個都係冇仔留落收尾個女人亦死、到復生時呢幾個人復生、個女人做邊個嘅妻、因爲呢七個都娶過佢咯。耶穌對佢哋話、你哋唔明白聖經亦唔知 神嘅權能、噉樣堂唔錯咩。回爲由死復生個時、冇嫁冇娶、照依天上嘅使者一樣。論及死者復生、你未讀過摩西書荊棘篇所載咩、卽係 神對摩西話我係亞伯拉罕嘅 神、雅各嘅 神、 神唔係死者嘅 神、乃係生者嘅 神、你哋大錯咯。

28 ¶ And one of the scribes came, and having heard them reasoning together, and perceiving that he had answered them well, asked him, Which is the first commandment of all?

29 And Jesus answered him, The first of all the commandments is, Hear, O Israel; The Lord our God is one Lord:

30 And thou shalt love the Lord thy God with all thy heart, and with all thy soul, and with all thy mind, and with all thy strength: this is the first commandment.

31 And the second is like, namely this, Thou shalt love thy neighbour as thyself. There is none other commandment greater than these.

32 And the scribe said unto him, Well, Master, thou hast said the truth: for there is one God; and there is none other but he:

33 And to love him with all the heart, and with all the understanding, and with all the soul, and with all the strength, and to love his neighbour as himself, is more than all whole burnt offerings and sacrifices.

34 And when Jesus saw that he answered discreetly, he said unto him, Thou art not far from the kingdom of God. And no man after that durst ask him any question.

○有一個讀書人嚟、既聽聞佢哋辯駁、又見耶穌對答得好、就問佢話、衆誡命之中、邊條係第一呢、耶穌答佢話第一條係話以色列人、你聽喇、主卽我哋嘅　神、係獨一嘅主呀。你哋應該盡心盡性盡意盡力嚟愛主你嘅　神、第二條係話當愛鄰舍猶如愛自己、冇別條誡命大得過呢兩條嘅略。讀書人對佢話好哩老師、你所講確係眞嘅因爲　神係獨一個、除佢之外冇別二個、愛鄰舍如愛自己、噉就好過各樣燔祭及別樣祭祀略。耶穌見佢應答得聰明、就對佢話你離　神國冇遠路、自此以後冇人敢再嚟盤問。

ST. MARK.

35 ¶ And Jesus answered and said, while he taught in the temple, How say the scribes that Christ is the Son of David?

36 For David himself said by the Holy Ghost, The LORD said to my Lord, Sit thou on my right hand, till I make thine enemies thy footstool.

37 David therefore himself calleth him Lord; and whence is he *then* his son? And the common people heard him gladly.

38 ¶ And he said unto them in his doctrine, Beware of the scribes, which love to go in long clothing, and *love* salutations in the marketplaces,

39 And the chief seats in the synagogues, and the uppermost rooms at feasts:

40 Which devour widows' houses, and for a pretence make long prayers: these shall receive greater damnation.

41 ¶ And Jesus sat over against the treasury, and beheld how the people cast money into the treasury: and many that were rich cast in much.

42 And there came a certain poor widow, and she threw in two mites, which make a farthing.

○耶穌喺殿裏教訓嘅話、讀書人、因何話基督係大闢嘅子孫呢。大闢被聖靈感動時、自己有話、主對我主話、你坐落我右便、等到我搣你嘅仇敵做你嘅腳踏凳大闢、既然稱基督做主、噉基督點樣係大闢嘅子孫呢、眾人好歡喜聽佢講。○耶穌教人之時又話、提防個的讀書人呀、佢地好著長衫行遊、歡喜人哋喺市上請佢安、與及喺會堂坐大位、喺筵席坐上位、但係佢吞寡婦嘅家財、假意做長新禱佢地受刑罰、是必更重呀。○耶穌對住殿嘅庫房坐見眾人揼銀簽題入庫有好多財主嘅人、簽題好多銀。又有一個窮寡婦嚟、簽題兩個錢、卽係一厘銀呧。

ST. MARK.

43 And he called *unto him* his disciples, and saith unto them, Verily I say unto you, That this poor widow hath cast more in, than all they which have cast into the treasury:

44 For all *they* did cast in of their abundance; but she of her want did cast in all that she had, *even* all her living.

CHAPTER 13.

AND as he went out of the temple, one of his disciples saith unto him, Master, see what manner of stones and what buildings *are here!*

2 And Jesus answering said unto him, Seest thou these great buildings? there shall not be left one stone upon another, that shall not be thrown down.

3 And as he sat upon the mount of Olives, over against the temple, Peter and James and John and Andrew asked him privately,

4 Tell us, when shall these things be? and what *shall be* the sign when all these things shall be fulfilled?

馬可第十三章

耶穌就叫門生嚟、對佢哋話、我實在話你知呢個窮寡婦所簽題、比較衆人簽入庫嘅重多呀因為衆人摣餘剩嘅嚟簽題但呢個窮婦雖不足亦摣哋所有嚟簽題卽係佢全賴嚟養口啊、

第十三章

耶穌出殿之時、有一個門生對佢話、老師、你睇吓呢啲石噉嘅殿宇吖耶穌對佢話、你見呢間大殿宇唖、將來冇一嚿石留番喺石之上、唔被毀拆嘅耶穌喺橄欖山上對住殿坐彼得雅各約翰安得烈靜靜問佢話請你話我哋知幾時有呢的事、而且呢的事一切將應驗時有乜兆頭呢。

ST. MARK.

5 And Jesus answering them began to say, Take heed lest any *man* deceive you:

6 For many shall come in my name, saying, I am *Christ*; and shall deceive many.

7 And when ye shall hear of wars and rumours of wars, be ye not troubled: for *such things* must needs be; but the end *shall* not *be* yet.

8 For nation shall rise against nation, and kingdom against kingdom: and there shall be earthquakes in divers places, and there shall be famines and troubles: these *are* the beginnings of sorrows.

9 But take heed to yourselves: for they shall deliver you up to councils; and in the synagogues ye shall be beaten: and ye shall be brought before rulers and kings for my sake, for a testimony against them.

10 And the gospel must first be published among all nations.

11 But when they shall lead *you*, and deliver you up, take no thought beforehand what ye shall speak, neither do ye premeditate: but whatsoever shall be given you in that hour, that speak ye: for it is not ye that speak, but the Holy Ghost.

12 Now the brother shall betray the brother to death, and the father the son; and children shall rise up against *their* parents, and shall cause them to be put to death.

耶穌對佢哋話、你哋謹慎、咪俾人迷惑呀。

將來有好多人、假冒我名嚟話我係基督、就迷惑好多人惟係你聽聞打仗與及打仗嘅風聲、唔使慌、呢的事是必有、但係末日未曾到呎。

民將攻打民國將攻打國、到處都有地震饑荒、呢的係災難嘅起首、你哋要謹慎自己因為人將解你哋過公會喺會堂裏打你、又為我解你企在大官國王面前嚟做佢嘅見證但係福音必先傳到萬國人、他拉你解官個時、唔使預先掛慮點樣講到個陣時、但凡賜過你講嘅你就嚟講因為唔係你自己講、乃係聖靈講呀。

兄弟將解兄弟去害死、父親待仔女亦起嚟攻擊父母、撼佢害死。

ST. MARK.

13 And ye shall be hated of all *men* for my name's sake: but he that shall endure unto the end, the same shall be saved.

14 ¶ But when ye shall see the abomination of desolation, spoken of by Daniel the prophet, standing where it ought not, (let him that readeth understand,) then let them that be in Judea flee to the mountains:

15 And let him that is on the housetop not go down into the house, neither enter *therein*, to take any thing out of his house:

16 And let him that is in the field not turn back again for to take up his garment.

17 But woe to them that are with child, and to them that give suck in those days!

18 And pray ye that your flight be not in the winter.

19 For *in* those days shall be affliction, such as was not from the beginning of the creation which God created unto this time, neither shall be.

20 And except that the Lord had shortened those days, no flesh should be saved: but for the elect's sake, whom he hath chosen, he hath shortened the days.

21 And then if any man shall say to you, Lo, here *is* Christ; or, lo, *he is* there; believe *him* not:

馬可第十三章

你哋爲我名、必受衆人憎惡、惟係忍耐到底嘅、佢必得救。○你哋睇見個的殘害可惡嘅物企在唔應企嘅地方、讀呢的書嘅要明白呀、個時喺猶太地嘅當要走上山喙屋上嘅人、唔好落去入屋攞什物出嚟、喺田嘅人、唔好回頭攞衣服。當個陣時懷胎及餵奶嘅女人有禍咯。你哋應該祈禱、免致喺冬天時避難呀、因爲當個陣時必有禍患、自從　神創造萬物、至到如今、未有嘅樣、後來亦冇嘅樣嘅。設使主唔減少個的日子、就凡有血氣嘅、冇一個得救咯、單係因佢所揀選嘅民、致減少個的日子個時若有人對你哋話、基督喺呢處、或喺個處、你唔好信。

St. Mark.

22 For false Christs and false prophets shall rise, and shall shew signs and wonders, to seduce, if *it were* possible, even the elect.

23 But take ye heed: behold, I have foretold you all things.

24 ¶ But in those days, after that tribulation, the sun shall be darkened, and the moon shall not give her light,

25 And the stars of heaven shall fall, and the powers that are in heaven shall be shaken.

26 And then shall they see the Son of man coming in the clouds with great power and glory.

27 And then shall he send his angels, and shall gather together his elect from the four winds, from the uttermost part of the earth to the uttermost part of heaven.

28 Now learn a parable of the fig tree: When her branch is yet tender, and putteth forth leaves, ye know that summer is near:

29 So ye in like manner, when ye shall see these things come to pass, know that it is nigh, *even* at the doors.

30 Verily I say unto you, that this generation shall not pass, till all these things be done.

31 Heaven and earth shall pass away: but my words shall not pass away.

馬可第十三章

三因為將來有的假基督假先知出嚟、做異蹟奇事、倘若誘惑得揀選嘅民就誘惑佢略。你哋要謹愼呀、我預先講啲過你聽略。當個陣時、個的禍患之後、熱頭將變黑暗、月色亦唔發光、星由天跌落天上各象都震動。個時佢哋就見人子挾大權能、大榮光、坐住雲落嚟、就打發天使聚埋四方所揀選嘅、自從地之極處至到天之極處。哋你哋見有呢的事、就知到人子係近嚟、到門口略。我實在話你知、呢個世代未曾過呢的事俱要成就嘅。天地必會廢壞、但我嘅說話、斷唔會廢壞。

ST. MARK.

32 ¶ But of that day and *that* hour knoweth no man, no, not the angels which are in heaven, neither the Son, but the Father.

33 Take ye heed, watch and pray: for ye know not when the time is.

34 *For the Son of man is* as a man taking a far journey, who left his house, and gave authority to his servants, and to every man his work, and commanded the porter to watch.

35 Watch ye therefore: for ye know not when the master of the house cometh, at even, or at midnight, or at the cock-crowing, or in the morning:

36 Lest coming suddenly he find you sleeping.

37 And what I say unto you I say unto all, Watch.

馬可第十三章

○惟係個的日期、個的時候、冇人知到、卽使天上使者與及人子都唔知獨係父知到呀。你哋要謹愼做醒祈禱、因爲你唔知個日期幾時到呀。好比一個人離開佢家、去遠處遊、搣權柄交過佢僕分開的事、俾各人做又吩咐看門嘅要做醒故此你哋應該做醒因爲唔知家主幾時嚟、或係挨晚、或係半夜、或係雞啼、或係天光。怕佢忽然嚟到遇着你哋瞓曉。我所話過你聽嘅、亦係話過衆人聽、要做醒呀。

ST. MARK.

第十四章

CHAPTER 14.

AFTER two days was *the feast of* the passover, and of unleavened bread: and the chief priests and the scribes sought how they might take him by craft, and put *him* to death.

2 But they said, Not on the feast *day,* lest there be an uproar of the people.

3 ¶ And being in Bethany, in the house of Simon the leper, as he sat at meat, there came a woman having an alabaster box of ointment of spikenard very precious; and she brake the box, and poured *it* on his head.

4 And there were some that had indignation within themselves, and said, Why was this waste of the ointment made?

5 For it might have been sold for more than three hundred pence, and have been given to the poor. And they murmured against her.

6 And Jesus said, Let her alone; why trouble ye her? she hath wrought a good work on me.

7 For ye have the poor with you always, and whensoever ye will ye may do them good: but me ye have not always.

過兩日、有個逾越節、卽係除酵節、衆祭司長及讀書人商畧用乜嘢詭計、捉耶穌嚟殺。但佢哋話唔好喺節期個時、怕百姓生亂。○耶穌喺伯大尼、癩西門嘅家坐在席上、有個女人、攞玉盒裝住至正至貴嘅香油嚟、揭開玉盒斟落耶穌頭上。有的人心唔歡喜話使乜咁花費個的香油呢。呢的香油可以賣得三十多兩銀、搣嚟施捨窮人、叵佢哋就執賣個女人。耶穌話由得佢喇、做乜攪擾佢呢、佢向我做一件好事呀、因爲個的窮人常時同你哋喺處、你想好看待佢、隨時都做得、但我唔係常時同你哋喺處。

68 ST. MARK.

8 She hath done what she could: she is come aforehand to anoint my body to the burying.

9 Verily I say unto you, Wheresoever this gospel shall be preached throughout the whole world, *this* also that she hath done shall be spoken of for a memorial of her.

10 ¶ And Judas Iscariot, one of the twelve, went unto the chief priests, to betray him unto them.

11 And when they heard *it*, they were glad, and promised to give him money. And he sought how he might conveniently betray him.

12 ¶ And the first day of unleavened bread, when they killed the passover, his disciples said unto him, Where wilt thou that we go and prepare that thou mayest eat the passover?

13 And he sendeth forth two of his disciples, and saith unto them, Go ye into the city, and there shall meet you a man bearing a pitcher of water: follow him.

14 And wheresoever he shall go in, say ye to the goodman of the house, The Master saith, Where is the guest-chamber, where I shall eat the passover with my disciples?

15 And he will shew you a large upper room furnished *and* prepared: there make ready for us.

馬可第十四章

⁸呢個女人盡佢嘅力嚟做、先搽香油搽我身、係預備我埋葬嘅呀。我實在話你哋知、通天下唔論喺邊處傳福音、都要講起呢個女人所做嘅嚟記念佢。十二門生之中、有一個加略人猶大去見眾祭司長、想賣耶穌過佢哋。佢哋聽聞好歡喜應承俾銀過佢、猶大就搵機會嚟賣耶穌。○除酵節第一日、劏逾越節羊仔個時、門生問耶穌、話你想我哋去邊處預備等你食逾越節嘅筵席呢。耶穌就打發兩個門生對佢話、你去入城必有一個人搂水埕嘅、過着你哋跟住佢入去、佢入嘅屋、你對家主話老師有話、我客房喺邊處等我共門生喺處食逾越節嘅筵席呢、佢必俾一間擺設齊整嘅大樓過你睇、你就喺個處為我哋預備喇。

St. Mark.

16 And his disciples went forth, and came into the city, and found as he had said unto them: and they made ready the passover.

17 And in the evening he cometh with the twelve.

18 And as they sat and did eat, Jesus said, Verily I say unto you, One of you which eateth with me shall betray me.

19 And they began to be sorrowful, and to say unto him one by one, *Is* it I? and another said, *Is* it I?

20 And he answered and said unto them, *It is* one of the twelve, that dippeth with me in the dish.

21 The Son of man indeed goeth, as it is written of him: but woe to that man by whom the Son of man is betrayed! good were it for that man if he had never been born.

22 ¶ And as they did eat, Jesus took bread, and blessed, and brake *it*, and gave to them, and said, Take, eat; this is my body.

23 And he took the cup, and when he had given thanks, he gave *it* to them: and they all drank of it.

24 And he said unto them, This is my blood of the new testament, which is shed for many.

門生就去入城、果然遇着照依耶穌對佢哋所講嘅、就預備逾越節嘅筵席。○到晚時、耶穌同十二門生嚟佢哋坐在席上食開個時、耶穌話我實在話你知你哋之中、有一個共我同食嘅是必賣我呀。門生就閉翳起嚟、逐一逐一問佢話係我咩、耶穌對佢哋話、十二門生之中、有一個同我擠手落碟嘅就係佢人子將過世係照經所指着佢嘅、但係賣人子個人有禍咯、個個人唔生出嚟重好。○食緊個時、耶穌攞餅祝謝、就擘開俾過門生話、你攞嚟呢嘅係我嘅身呀又攞隻杯感謝、俾過門生、大衆就飲嘵。耶穌對佢哋話呢嘅係我嘅血、係新約嘅血、為衆人流嘅。

25 Verily I say unto you, I will drink no more of the fruit of the vine, until that day that I drink it new in the kingdom of God.

26 ¶ And when they had sung a hymn, they went out into the mount of Olives.

27 And Jesus saith unto them, All ye shall be offended because of me this night: for it is written, I will smite the Shepherd, and the sheep shall be scattered.

28 But after that I am risen, I will go before you into Galilee.

29 But Peter said unto him, Although all shall be offended, yet *will* not I.

30 And Jesus saith unto him, Verily I say unto thee, That this day, *even* in this night, before the cock crow twice, thou shalt deny me thrice.

31 But he spake the more vehemently, If I should die with thee, I will not deny thee in any wise. Likewise also said they all.

32 And they came to a place which was named Gethsemane: and he saith to his disciples, Sit ye here, while I shall pray.

33 And he taketh with him Peter and James and John, and began to be sore amazed, and to be very heavy;

34 And saith unto them, My soul is exceeding sorrowful unto death: tarry ye here, and watch.

我實在話你哋知、我唔再飲菩提樹所生嘅、等到個日我喺　神國、致飲新嘅咯。但佢哋唱曉一首詩、就去到橄欖山耶穌對佢哋話、你哋衆人必厭棄我因爲聖經有話、我將打個牧人、啲就羣羊散唨咯。但我復生之後、必先過你哋去到加利利彼得對佢話、衆人雖然厭棄你、我必唔係耶穌答佢話我實在話你知今晚第二次雞啼之先、你是必三次唔認我。但彼得又極力話、卽使共你同死我斷冇話唔認你、衆人亦係噉樣講去到一嗱地方叫做客西馬尼耶穌對門生話、你哋坐倒呢處等我祈禱。於是帶住彼得雅各約翰同埋自己行、就好驚慌好悲切對佢哋話、我心閉翳到死咯、你哋喺呢處等候、又要做醒呀。

ST. MARK.　　　馬可第十四章

35 And he went forward a little, and fell on the ground, and prayed that, if it were possible, the hour might pass from him.

36 And he said, Abba, Father, all things *are* possible unto thee; take away this cup from me: nevertheless, not what I will, but what thou wilt.

37 And he cometh, and findeth them sleeping, and saith unto Peter, Simon, sleepest thou? couldest not thou watch one hour?

38 Watch ye and pray, lest ye enter into temptation. The spirit truly *is* ready, but the flesh *is* weak.

39 And again he went away, and prayed, and spake the same words.

40 And when he returned, he found them asleep again, (for their eyes were heavy,) neither wist they what to answer him.

41 And he cometh the third time, and saith unto them, Sleep on now, and take *your* rest: it is enough, the hour is come; behold, the Son of man is betrayed into the hands of sinners.

42 Rise up, let us go; lo, he that betrayeth me is at hand.

三五 佢就行前幾步、噗到地處祈禱話、呢個時候可以免得就求喇。

三六 又話、亞爸父呀你係無所不能求呢隻杯離開我、但唔係從我所想哋、惟係從你所想呢。

三七 又番嚟、見門生瞓著、就對彼得話、西門你瞓覺咩、你不能做醒半個時辰咩。

三八 做醒呀、祈禱呀免致入迷惑呀、你心係情願、但身體軟弱咯。

三九 又再去祈禱、說話同一樣咯。

四十 又番嚟、見門生又瞓著、因係眼倦呀、佢哋都唔知點樣回答耶穌。

四一 又第三次番嚟、對佢哋話你哋可以瞓覺安息咯、罷咯時候到嘑、人子係賣過罪人嘅手嘑。

四二 起身嘑、我哋要去咯、賣我個人嚟近咯。

72 ST. MARK.

43 ¶ And immediately, while he yet spake, cometh Judas, one of the twelve, and with him a great multitude with swords and staves, from the chief priests and the scribes and the elders.

44 And he that betrayed him had given them a token, saying, Whomsoever I shall kiss, that same is he; take him, and lead *him* away safely.

45 And as soon as he was come, he goeth straightway to him, and saith, Master, Master; and kissed him.

46 ¶ And they laid their hands on him, and took him.

47 And one of them that stood by drew a sword, and smote a servant of the high priest, and cut off his ear.

48 And Jesus answered and said unto them, Are ye come out, as against a thief, with swords and *with* staves to take me?

49 I was daily with you in the temple teaching, and ye took me not: but the Scriptures must be fulfilled.

50 And they all forsook him and fled.

51 And there followed him a certain young man, having a linen cloth cast about *his* naked *body;* and the young men laid hold on him:

52 And he left the linen cloth, and fled from them naked.

馬可第十四章

○講緊個時、十二門生之中有個猶大同埋好多人嚟揸刀揸棍喺衆祭司長讀書人長老個處嚟、賣耶穌個人先俾個暗號過佢哋話、我所親嘴嘅、就係佢略、捉倒要子細拉佢去呀。已經嚟到、卽刻行埋耶穌處話、夫子就同佢親嘴、嘅人就落手捉耶穌。○喺側邊企處嘅有一個人拔出把劍斬大祭司長嘅僕削用佢隻耳、耶穌對衆人話、你哋揸刀揸棍嚟捉我好似捉賊噉咩、我日日共你喺殿裏敎人、你哋唔捉我但哋係令聖經所載嘅得應驗略。門生個個離開耶穌走去、有一個少年嘅人佢身獨係摟住一塊蔴布嚟跟耶穌個的人捉住佢、佢就褪用個塊蔴布、赤身走去。

ST. MARK.

53 ¶ And they led Jesus away to the high priest: and with him were assembled all the chief priests and the elders and the scribes.

54 And Peter followed him afar off, even into the palace of the high priest: and he sat with the servants, and warmed himself at the fire.

55 And the chief priests and all the council sought for witness against Jesus to put him to death; and found none.

56 For many bare false witness against him, but their witness agreed not together.

57 And there arose certain, and bare false witness against him, saying,

58 We heard him say, I will destroy this temple that is made with hands, and within three days I will build another made without hands.

59 But neither so did their witness agree together.

60 And the high priest stood up in the midst, and asked Jesus, saying, Answerest thou nothing? what *is it which* these witness against thee?

61 But he held his peace, and answered nothing. Again the high priest asked him, and said unto him, Art thou the Christ, the Son of the Blessed?

○衆人拉耶穌去個大祭司長面前、衆祭司長及長老讀書人都齊集。彼得遠遠跟住耶穌入到大祭司長嘅院共個嘅差役坐處焙火衆祭司長及全公會嘅人、搵見證據告耶穌想害死佢、但係唔搵得倒。因爲好多人做假證告佢、但係所證嘅唔相合。又有幾個人起身捏假證據告佢話、我哋聽過佢講話、呢間殿係人手所做嘅、我將拆曉佢、三日內起過一間、唔係人手所做嘅。但佢哋所證亦唔相合。大祭司長喺衆人之中起身問耶穌話、你冇說話回答咩、呢的人做證告你也嘢呢。耶穌總唔出聲答佢、大祭司長再問佢話、你係可讀頌者之子基督唔係呢。

62 And Jesus said, I am: and ye shall see the Son of man sitting on the right hand of power, and coming in the clouds of heaven.

63 Then the high priest rent his clothes, and saith, What need we any further witnesses?

64 Ye have heard the blasphemy: what think ye? And they all condemned him to be guilty of death.

65 And some began to spit on him, and to cover his face, and to buffet him, and to say unto him, Prophesy: and the servants did strike him with the palms of their hands.

66 ¶ And as Peter was beneath in the palace, there cometh one of the maids of the high priest:

67 And when she saw Peter warming himself, she looked upon him, and said, And thou also wast with Jesus of Nazareth.

68 But he denied, saying, I know not, neither understand I what thou sayest. And he went out into the porch; and the cock crew.

69 And a maid saw him again, and began to say to them that stood by, This is one of them.

⁶²耶穌話、我係略、你哋將來見人子、坐在全能者嘅右便、駕住天雲落嚟呀。大祭司長就擘爛自己衣服話、我哋重要搵乜嘢見證呢、你哋包經聽聞佢褻瀆嘅話哩、你哋意思點呢、眾人擬佢應得死罪。⁶⁵有的遮住佢面搣拳頭打佢話、你係先知試話出乜誰叮個的差役又搣手掌摑佢。彼得喺下院處、大祭司長有一個妹仔嚟、見彼得焙火、就睇住佢話、你平素都係同埋𠊎撒勒耶穌嘅、⁶⁸彼得唔認就話我唔知亦唔曉你講乜嘢、敵就出去行到大門口嘅簷邊、雞就啼、⁶⁹個個妹仔見佢、再對企倒側邊嘅人話、呢個人係同佢哋一黨㗎、但彼得又唔認。

ST. MARK.

70 And he denied it again. And a little after, they that stood by said again to Peter, Surely thou art *one* of them: for thou art a Galilean, and thy speech agreeth *thereto*.

71 But he began to curse and to swear, *saying*, I know not this man of whom ye speak.

72 And the second time the cock crew. And Peter called to mind the word that Jesus said unto him, Before the cock crow twice, thou shalt deny me thrice. And when he thought thereon, he wept.

CHAPTER 15.

AND straightway in the morning the chief priests held a consultation with the elders and scribes and the whole council, and bound Jesus, and carried *him* away, and delivered *him* to Pilate.

2 And Pilate asked him, Art thou the King of the Jews? And he answering said unto him, Thou sayest *it*.

3 And the chief priests accused him of many things; but he answered nothing.

4 And Pilate asked him again, saying, Answerest thou nothing? behold how many things they witness against thee.

馬可第十五章

耶有耐企倒側嘅人、再對彼得話你真係同佢哋一黨嘅咯、因為你係加利利人呀。彼得就呪詛而且誓願話你哋所講個個人、我唔識佢呀。雞即時第二次啼、彼得記起耶穌所講話第二次雞啼之先你必三回唔認我、想着呢句說話就喊起嚟。

第十五章

到朝早個時、衆祭司長及長老讀書人共全公會嘅人、大家斟酌、就綁起耶穌、搋佢交過彼拉多。彼拉多問佢話你係猶太人嘅王咩、耶穌答佢話、你講得着咯、衆祭司長搕好多事嚟告佢、彼拉多再問佢話、你睇佢哋搕咁多事嚟告你、你冇的對答咩、

St. MARK.

5 But Jesus yet answered nothing; so that Pilate marvelled.

6 Now at *that* feast he released unto them one prisoner, whomsoever they desired.

7 And there was *one* named Barabbas, *which lay* bound with them that had made insurrection with him, who had committed murder in the insurrection.

8 And the multitude crying aloud began to desire *him to do* as he had ever done unto them.

9 But Pilate answered them, saying, Will ye that I release unto you the King of the Jews?

10 For he knew that the chief priests had delivered him for envy.

11 But the chief priests moved the people, that he should rather release Barabbas unto them.

12 And Pilate answered and said again unto them, What will ye then that I shall do *unto him* whom ye call the King of the Jews?

13 And they cried out again, Crucify him.

14 Then Pilate said unto them, Why, what evil hath he done? And they cried out the more exceedingly, Crucify him.

馬可第十五章

⁵但耶穌總唔出聲、故此彼拉多見出奇。○⁶當呢個節期、照依常例、總督要放一個犯人、係任從衆人所求嘅。⁷有一人名叫巴拉巴、共個的作反嘅人同埋綁住佢哋作反之時、也曾殺人。衆人就大聲叫、求總督照例嚟做彼拉多對衆人話。⁹你想我放猶太人嘅王過你唔呢。因爲佢知到衆祭司長妒忌耶穌、故此解佢嚟呀。¹¹衆祭司長聳動百姓、求總督寧可放巴拉巴俾佢。¹²彼拉多再答衆人話、噉樣、你哋所稱猶太人王嘅、我要點樣處置佢呢。¹³衆人再大聲話、釘佢落十字架喇。彼拉多對佢哋話佢做過乜嘢惡事呢。衆人越發大聲叫、釘佢落十字架喇。

St. Mark. 馬可第十五章 77

15 ¶ And *so* Pilate, willing to content the people, released Barabbas unto them, and delivered Jesus, when he had scourged *him*, to be crucified.

16 And the soldiers led him away into the hall, called Pretorium; and they call together the whole band.

17 And they clothed him with purple, and platted a crown of thorns, and put it about his *head*,

18 And began to salute him, Hail, King of the Jews!

19 And they smote him on the head with a reed, and did spit upon him, and bowing *their* knees worshipped him.

20 And when they had mocked him, they took off the purple from him, and put his own clothes on him, and led him out to crucify him.

21 And they compel one Simon a Cyrenian, who passed by, coming out of the country, the father of Alexander and Rufus, to bear his cross.

22 And they bring him unto the place Golgotha, which is, being interpreted, The place of a skull.

23 And they gave him to drink wine mingled with myrrh: but he received *it* not.

24 And when they had crucified him, they parted his garments, casting lots upon them, what every man should take.

25 And it was the third hour, and they crucified him.

彼拉多想安百姓嘅心、就放巴拉巴俾過佢哋、又鞭打耶穌、交過人去釘佢落十字架、○個的兵拉耶穌入去院內、即係公堂就會埋通營嘅人、又撳荊棘結成冕戴土佢頭。就問佢安嘅話猶太人嘅王平安叮。又撳條蘆荻打佢頭俾口水唾佢身跪倒處拜佢戲弄完、就脫曉個件紫色袍共佢著番自己嘅衣服拉佢出去釘落十字架、有個古利奈人名叫西門、即係亞力山大及魯孚嘅父親、喺田間嚟經過個處眾人強佢孭住耶穌嘅十字架、佢哋帶耶穌到一𡍲地方名叫各各他、繙譯即係枯顱頭處就撳沒藥嘅酒俾佢、但耶穌唔受嘅。就釘佢落十字架、又分開佢衣服、執籌睇吓誰得邊份。釘佢在十字架個時、正係辰時尾。

78　ST. MARK.

26 And the superscription of his accusation was written over, THE KING OF THE JEWS.

27 And with him they crucify two thieves; the one on his right hand, and the other on his left.

28 And the Scripture was fulfilled, which saith, And he was numbered with the transgressors.

29 And they that passed by railed on him, wagging their heads, and saying, Ah, thou that destroyest the temple, and buildest *it* in three days,

30 Save thyself, and come down from the cross.

31 Likewise also the chief priests mocking said among themselves with the scribes, He saved others; himself he cannot save.

32 Let Christ the king of Israel descend now from the cross, that we may see and believe. And they that were crucified with him reviled him.

33 And when the sixth hour was come, there was darkness over the whole land until the ninth hour.

34 And at the ninth hour Jesus cried with a loud voice, saying, Eloi, Eloi, lama sabachthani? which is, being interpreted, My God, my God, why hast thou forsaken me?

35 And some of them that stood by, when they heard *it*, said, Behold, he calleth Elias.

馬可第十五章

佢上頭有條犯罪嘅標、寫出話猶太人嘅王、又有兩個賊同埋釘落十字架、一在佢左便、一在佢右便嘅。就應曉聖經所寫、人算佢係罪犯之中嘅人個句咯。經過嘅人藝瀆佢、吭吓個頭話、咳、你唔拆個間殿、三日內又起番、如今該救自己、喺十字架落嚟哩。衆祭司長及讀書人亦係噉樣戲弄佢、大家相講話、佢救得別人、唔救得己呀。以色列王基督、如今應喺十字架落嚟、等我哋睇見就信略、同埋釘嘅賊亦怒罵佢。○自正午時至未時尾、全地黑暗、未時屎個陣耶穌大聲叫話、吚唎吚唎啦嗎嘞嘅吠呢、繙譯卽係我嘅 神做乜遺落我呢、嘅側邊企嘅有的人聽見就話佢叫以利亞嘅。

ST. MARK.

36 And one ran and filled a sponge full of vinegar, and put *it* on a reed, and gave him to drink, saying, Let alone; let us see whether Elias will come to take him down.

37 And Jesus cried with a loud voice, and gave up the ghost.

38 And the vail of the temple was rent in twain from the top to the bottom.

39 ¶ And when the centurion, which stood over against him, saw that he so cried out, and gave up the ghost, he said, Truly this man was the Son of God.

40 There were also women looking on afar off: among whom was Mary Magdalene, and Mary the mother of James the less and of Joses, and Salome;

41 Who also, when he was in Galilee, followed him, and ministered unto him; and many other women which came up with him unto Jerusalem.

42 ¶ And now when the even was come, because it was the preparation, that is, the day before the sabbath,

43 Joseph of Arimathea, an honourable counsellor, which also waited for the kingdom of God, came, and went in boldly unto Pilate, and craved the body of Jesus.

三六有個人走去搣水泡浸落醋處、扎在蘆荻上、遞過佢飲話、由得佢嚇、我哋睇以利亞嚟、攞佢落嚟唔吖。耶穌大叫一聲氣就斷曉。殿裏布帳、自上至下、裂開兩截、有個百夫長企在耶穌對面、睇見佢嘅樣大聲斷氣就話呢個人、真係 神之子咯、又有女人、隔遠望住其中有抹大拉嘅馬利亞共年少雅各約西嘅母親馬利亞、與及撒羅米、卽一係耶穌喺加利利個時跟從服事佢嘅、更有好多女人、係同佢上耶路撒冷嘅。個日係預備嘅日子、卽係安息前一日、已經挨晚時候、有個亞利馬太人約瑟嚟、佢係尊貴嘅議士仰慕 神國嘅、放膽入去見彼拉多求耶穌嘅屍。

ST. MARK.

44 And Pilate marvelled if he were already dead: and calling *unto him* the centurion, he asked him whether he had been any while dead.

45 And when he knew *it* of the centurion, he gave the body to Joseph.

46 And he bought fine linen, and took him down, and wrapped him in the linen, and laid him in a sepulchre which was hewn out of a rock, and rolled a stone unto the door of the sepulchre.

47 And Mary Magdalene and Mary *the mother* of Jesus beheld where he was laid.

CHAPTER 16.

AND when the sabbath was past, Mary Magdalene, and Mary the *mother* of James, and Salome, had bought sweet spices, that they might come and anoint him.

2 And very early in the morning, the first *day* of the week, they came unto the sepulchre at the rising of the sun.

3 And they said among themselves, Who shall roll us away the stone from the door of the sepulchre?

4 And when they looked, they saw that the stone was rolled away: for it was very great.

馬可第十六章

彼拉多詫異耶穌已經死曉、就叫百總嚟問過佢死曉幾耐呢。既問明百把總就俾個屍過約瑟、約瑟嚟曉幼細麻布、就攞個屍落嚟、將麻布包好、葬在墳墓呢個墳墓係磐石鑿開嘅、佢又轆一礓石、塞住墳墓口、抹大拉嘅馬利亞與及約西嘅母親馬利亞都見葬佢個噲地方略。

第十六章

安息日已經過、抹大拉嘅馬利亞共雅各嘅母親馬利亞與及撒羅米、買曉香料、想嚟搽耶穌嘅屍。七日期之第一日、清早、熱頭初出個時佢哋嚟到墳墓處、大家相講話也誰替我哋轆開墳口個嚿石呢、因爲個嚿石好大呀。但一望就睇見個嚿石已經轆開、

St. Mark.

5 And entering into the sepulchre, they saw a young man sitting on the right side, clothed in a long white garment; and they were affrighted.

6 And he saith unto them, Be not affrighted: ye seek Jesus of Nazareth, which was crucified: he is risen; he is not here: behold the place where they laid him.

7 But go your way, tell his disciples and Peter that he goeth before you into Galilee: there shall ye see him, as he said unto you.

8 And they went out quickly, and fled from the sepulchre; for they trembled and were amazed: neither said they any thing to any *man*; for they were afraid.

9 ¶ Now when *Jesus* was risen early the first *day* of the week, he appeared first to Mary Magdalene, out of whom he had cast seven devils.

10 *And* she went and told them that had been with him, as they mourned and wept.

11 And they, when they had heard that he was alive, and had been seen of her, believed not.

馬可第十六章

⁵入到墳裏、見一個年少嘅人、坐在右便、身著白衫、個的女人就好驚慌。⁶年少嘅對佢哋話唔使慌、你哋揾釘十字架個拿撒勒耶穌、嘅、佢已經復生、唔喺呢處咯、你哋睇吓葬佢嘅地方可但係去話過佢哋個門生及彼得知、耶穌先過你哋去加利利喺個處一路走好靈好慌一句都唔講過人聽、因爲佢驚慌呀。○七日期之第一日朝早時、耶穌既復生先見出嚟俾抹大拉嘅馬利亞見、卽係從前耶穌喺佢身趕過七隻鬼個個平日共耶穌同伴嘅人、正在嗰處悲哀啼哭呢個女人去話過佢哋知衆人聽聞耶穌復生俾呢個女人睇見就唔信。

82 ST. MARK.

12 ¶ After that he appeared in another form unto two of them, as they walked, and went into the country.

13 And they went and told *it* unto the residue: neither believed they them.

14 ¶ Afterward he appeared unto the eleven as they sat at meat, and upbraided them with their unbelief and hardness of heart, because they believed not them which had seen him after he was risen.

15 And he said unto them, Go ye into all the world, and preach the gospel to every creature.

16 He that believeth and is baptized shall be saved; but he that believeth not shall be damned.

17 And these signs shall follow them that believe; In my name shall they cast out devils; they shall speak with new tongues;

18 They shall take up serpents; and if they drink any deadly thing, it shall not hurt them; they shall lay hands on the sick, and they shall recover.

19 ¶ So then, after the Lord had spoken unto them, he was received up into heaven, and sat on the right hand of God.

20 And they went forth, and preached everywhere, the Lord working with *them*, and confirming the word with signs following. Amen.

馬可第十六章

○後來門生之中、有兩個落鄉行路之時、耶穌變轉容貌、現出過佢哋見。呢兩個人、去講過其餘嘅門生聽佢哋亦唔信。○到尾後十一個門生嚟席上坐之時、耶穌又現出嚟、責成佢哋唔信及硬心、因佢哋唔信見過佢復生嘅人呀。○耶穌對佢哋話、你哋去通天下、傳講福音過萬人聽、而受洗禮嘅必得救、唔信嘅必要定罪。信嘅到處必有異蹟做出、即係托我名趕鬼、能講別國土談、又可以揸蛇、或飲毒物都冇損傷佢、手按吓病人佢病就好番。○路主耶穌共佢哋講完就升上天坐在 神右便門生出去各處傳道、主帮助佢哋、誠異蹟嚟做道理嘅見證。

www.ingramcontent.com/pod-product-compliance
Lightning Source LLC
Chambersburg PA
CBHW020318090426
42735CB00009B/1361